Paris

Paris Larousse

Text by J.M. Carzou
Translation by Winifred Porter

Librairie Larousse
17, rue du Montparnasse
75006 Paris

editorial office: M. F. Vaudois
art directors: F. Longuépée and H. Serres-Cousiné
iconography: F. Arnault and A.M. Moyse
proof-reading: B. Dauphin and M.P. Gachet

Contents

Introductory chapter, *page 7*

An inventory of Paris
Its island cradle, *page 13*
Left bank...right bank, *page 25*
Louvre-Concorde, *page 31*
The City Centre, *page 43*
The faubourg Saint-Germain, *page 55*
Back on the Champs-Elysées, *page 73*
The Opéra, *page 83*
On the Grands Boulevards, *page 89*
The ancient villages of Paris, *page 97*
From Grenelle to Passy, *page 101*
The heights of Paris, *page 107*

The three ages of Paris
"Beneath the pavements, a beach...", *page 116*
From Haussmann to Bienvenüe, *page 118*
Towards the year 2000, *page 121*

Living in Paris
A permanent world fair, *page 128*
Some other views of Paris, *page 132*
A few special addresses, *page 134*
Paris by night, *page 135*

Some maps of Paris: *pages 142 and 143*

Already the plane is losing height
as it makes its final approach into Orly or Roissy-Charles-de-Gaulle.
"Ladies and Gentlemen, in a few moments we shall be landing.
Please fasten your safety belts and put out all cigarettes."
As the wheels touch the ground the voice of the air-hostess
adds a few last, magic words:
"Welcome to Paris."
Magic words, certainly, for that brief message produces
the same electric effect on travellers from all over the world as they hear it.
Their eyes light up with excitement at her very name,
for Paris is the realization of every dream and her fascination is universal.
Fascination, for no other word can even begin
to echo exactly the enchantment of those two short syllables:

Paris

Day is breaking over Paris... the Eiffel Tower stands out against the dawn sky as we approach the city from the west...

Fluctuat nec mergitur — the motto of Paris on her coat of arms..

8

PARIS, REINE DU MONDE! runs one popular song. *Paris, qui sera toujours Paris* runs another. And certainly over the centuries she has acquired a glory which still today shines out undiminished. Times have changed, other major capitals have sprung up in the world, France is no longer the great imperial power of days gone by, some of the old spirit of Paris may have gone, but she is still the unchallenged queen among cities, an unrivalled beauty who has aroused overwhelming passion in the hearts and minds of her admirers and an all-consuming hatred in those of her enemies.

Three times in less than a century and a half — and there was almost a fourth time in the autumn of 1914 — German armies came and occupied the city, this "corrupt Babylon" to which they were drawn as if despite themselves, bent upon razing her to the ground, destroying her for ever. But how do you destroy a legend! How can you exorcize an undying spirit?

The Arc de Triomphe, like a vigilant night-watchman, has been alight all night in the heart of the sleeping plain.

10 The invasions continue, but the invading armies are now armies of eager tourists flocking in ever-increasing numbers, magnetically drawn to this magic paradise nestling in the sweep of the Seine. Yesterday's tourists became today's residents. They came from the provinces first, leaving the countryside and settling in the capital, and they now form the bulk of the population of Paris. Then came the foreign visitors, for whom life would not be complete without at least one visit to this queen of cities. So over the centuries what was once a little island settlement in the river Seine has grown into the great city Paris is today. Like the ripples on a pond, ever-increasing circles of houses and flats, streets and monuments have gradually spread out into the countryside round that original island, surrounded like Rome by the circle of its seven hills.

But our Queen of Cities has no time to ponder over all that past history. She is far too busy trying to cope with the insane maelstrom of activity which daily assails her, created by the government's passion for centralization wich has made Paris the pivot round which the whole of French life revolves.

Let us look at a few revealing statistics: Paris covers 0.2 % of the total area of France, yet into that tiny proportion of her territory 4 % of her entire population is crammed. In other words there are on average more than 20,000 people per square kilometre in the city overall, and anything up to 50,000 in the most densely populated industrial suburbs on the perimeter of Paris. As a direct result, Paris practically monopolizes the important social and decision-making centres, the banks and business houses. Another consequence is the pattern of France's transport system, for all her major roads and railway lines radiate from the capital. And thus it is that every day, especially at the morning peak hours, Paris is crammed almost to the point of suffocation with thousands of people who pour in by train or metro or

A quiet corner of Montmartre, and the funicular which takes the less energetic visitor to the Sacré-Cœur at the top of the hill.

car to join the thousands who already live there. They stream out from every metro exit, every railway station, every car park and bus stop and disappear like so many ants into the shops and offices, the factories and restaurants of this fantastic city, which rivals New York or Tokyo in its frenzied activity.

But we are seeing it all from the air as our plane loses height and prepares to land. There, stretched out below us like an enormous map, lies the city. High above the two ring-roads — the *boulevards extérieurs* and the *boulevard périphérique* —, which today mark the outer limits of the city proper, we instantly appreciate both the density and the richness of Paris. All the hallmarks of modern urban development are clearly distinguishable: the tightly interwoven network of roads, the familiar green of the parks, which are all the more noticeable because they are comparatively few and far between in this dense grey jungle of buildings, and finally as we drop nearer, the famous monuments themselves. We pick them out one after the other like so many old friends: the Arc de Triomphe, the Eiffel Tower, the Invalides, the Sacré-Cœur and a host of others. They seem to float upon the surface of this sea of grey stone, from which there also suddenly bursts the

multi-coloured mass of the Pompidou Centre, the latest phenomenon in this ever-changing world. Even at night it is all there to greet us, a dazzling carpet of glittering lights spread out beneath our gaze.

Now though, it is time to take our bearings again for we have touched down at the airport and, seen from the ground, those myriad lights merge into a magnificent orange glow, visible for miles around and lighting up the night sky like a second sun. In the morning light, everything is back to normal and, just before the broad ribbon of the road from the airport plunges into the heart of this great metropolis, we get a last panoramic

view of the city, as our eye moves from the Eiffel Tower down by the river, to the Sacré-Cœur crowning the heights of Montmartre.

Long ago, when the road was the only means of access, how many men must have trodden its path, counting every milestone as they left their native provinces to seek work in Paris! The fascination of the great city lured them and drove them on, and in any case there was no longer work for them in the countryside once the relentless machine of centralization took over and brought everything to Paris. The young Rousseau who fled there from his native Geneva in 1741 never really managed to escape

The metro at dawn... even the trains sometimes stop to admire the beauty of the Seine as they cross the Bir-Hakeim viaduct between Grenelle and Passy.

A typical Paris bistro... row upon row of glasses against the mirrored walls, and a few regulars at the bar.

This statue of "Liberty taking flight and breaking its chains" stands symbolically on top of the column in the place de la Bastille which commemorates the 1830 revolution.

from her thrall, and even if twenty years later, in his *Confessions,* he appeared to view her with a more critical eye, we are still aware that he was one more victim of that fatal fascination which Paris never fails to exert.

Perhaps we should beware in case she keeps us prisoners in her chains too! But that is a risk we must take so, like the hero of Offenbach's *La Vie Parisienne* who sings *Je serai votre guide dans la ville splendide,* the following pages of this book will be your guide. And that is no mean task! There is so much to say about these 105 square kilometres which in the course of two thousand years of history have grown from a tiny island in the Seine into twenty *arrondissements* and two large stretches of forest.

We shall try not to linger too long over the traditional places of interest for they have been so exhaustively dealt with elsewhere. We are going to try to understand something of a civilisation which has become inextricably intertwined with its place of birth. So we shall attempt to follow the city's own convoluted pattern of development from the island in the river where it was born, outwards to its present perimeter. We shall go from the first *arrondissement* right round to the last, exploring one district after another — they will not all be equally rich but in each there will be something to discover. We shall climb hill after hill, find one treasure after another, often following the whims of the great river which seems unwilling to continue its journey to the sea as it twists and turns and turns again round its treasure.

Then having made an inventory of all the wonderful things we have seen, would it not be pleasant to glance back — out of curiosity rather than nostalgia — at those periods when, sometimes gradually, sometimes more quickly, sometimes even brutally, the town has changed in some significant way, evolved, enriched its fabric of buildings and varied architectural styles? For the face of Paris is always changing. We are usually only aware of the most recent of these changes for they are taking place under our very eyes. The rest are all too easily forgotten, for the dust of centuries has settled over them. But traces of the past still live on and combine to evoke a sense of continuity, a feeling of immortality. Paris is a fabulous multi-faceted exhibition, a permanent one, offering us night and day not only things to see, but also things to eat, to drink, to read, to experience, to laugh at, to love... In short, it offers us the privilege of living and enjoying life in the midst of the most extraordinary concentration of riches on this planet. The mediaeval walls have gone, the fortifications of later centuries have been razed to the ground, the *octroi* is no longer levied at the gates. There are no gates, no barriers now; there is nothing to hinder the motorist as he sweeps along the broad avenues which lead to the heart of the city. Today, Paris is wide open to everyone, ready to welcome all those who admire and love her. ∎

Early morning on the S.N.C.F.

1

an inventory of Paris

its island cradle

L ET US IMAGINE PARIS as a circle with the Ile de la Cité at its centre. It needs little imagination to do so, for, seen on a map, the city is indeed roughly shaped like a circle. History and the pattern of the city's growth reinforce this notion, for it was on this island at the very heart of the city that the first inhabitants settled.

Once upon a time, more than two thousand years ago, one of the many scattered tribes who roamed the countryside of ancient Gaul landed on this tiny wooded island in the river Seine and settled there. Their village was called Lutetia and the tribe were known as the Parisii. In the course of time, when the

The sun rises over the Ile de la Cité lighting up Notre-Dame and the towers of the Conciergerie.

◄ *The Ile de la Cité seen from the pont du Carrousel in the early morning light. The arches of the pont Neuf seem to anchor the island to the banks of the Seine.*

Notre-Dame and the Ile de la Cité recede into the shadow as the sun lights up the 17th century houses of its sister island the Ile Saint-Louis.

18 Romans conquered Gaul — for conquer it they certainly did, whatever Astérix may have led you to believe — Lutetia was called after the Parisii and became... Paris!

Later on when the country was in the hands of invading barbarian hordes, the Gauls and their Roman masters, the latter's domination now seriously threatened, worked together to fortify the island and protect their town. For the infant Paris, these ramparts were to mark her original boundary, enclosing a central core around which, in a series of ever-widening circles, the city has continued to grow, in defiance of all who attempted to destroy her.

The view from the air — or a glance at the plan of Paris — shows how much like a ship at anchor in the river this island looks. Moored to both banks by bridges, its prow pointing proudly downstream towards the sea, it must have caught the imagination of its mediaeval rulers in just the same way, for they chose as their coat of arms the emblem of a majestic ship floating on stylized waves, an emblem which all through the centuries has reflected the pride, the boldness of a city which nothing has been able to subdue for long.

That small ship has long outgrown its first modest anchorage, but it is still afloat, and despite countless trials and tribulations, internal upheavals and foreign storms which have battered against its bulwarks, it has lived up to its proud motto: *fluctuat nec mergitur.* It has indeed proved unsinkable.

And if for the voyage of discovery we are about to make to the furthest corners of Paris, I have chosen the term "inventory", nowhere does it apply better than to our original ship, now peacefully at anchor and loaded with its cargo of priceless architectural jewels. As we make our way through the narrow gangways of its streets, we make discovery after discovery, finding treasures crammed into every available inch of space. And, apart from a few later additions and some

A leafy riverside walk and the footbridge which links the two islands in the Seine.

major restoration work in the 19th century, it has all been here since the Middle Ages or even earlier — the Palais de Justice, the Conciergerie, the Sainte-Chapelle, the place Dauphine and Notre-Dame, the unchallenged queen who dominates them all by the sheer mass of her presence. But still the list is far from complete. We must not forget less spectacular treasures like the ancient streets in the shadow of the cathedral with their mediaeval houses where life still goes on as it always has done. Nor must we forget those other treasures, older by far, which recent excavations have brought to light. Our ship is a meeting place of the centuries and throughout its length we find, in strange juxtaposition, everything from Roman remains to the souvenir shops frequented by today's tourists.

Then where shall we begin? In the west of the island, perhaps? If so, we shall disembark in front of that imposing complex of buildings, the Palais de Justice. Its lofty, sheer walls extend from one side of the island to the other, occupying its whole width and even spilling over on to the far side of the boulevard which bears its name, for you can regularly see lawyers in their flowing robes standing patiently at the pavement edge among the anonymous crowds of ordinary passers-by, waiting to cross over

the busy street from one courtroom to another.

But, impressive as this enormous pile of buildings is from the outside, it is inside, behind those lofty unscalable walls that the real treasures are to be found. The great towers which flank the Conciergerie cannot fail to evoke the atmosphere of the original fortress and the first royal palace built on the site. But the finest treasures are inside, and a visit to the old part of the Palace is like a walk through the Middle Ages. One passes from the once crowded dungeons of the old prison to the incomparable stained-glass windows of the Sainte-Chapelle with its graceful Gothic spire. A superb flight of broad stone steps at the western end of the Palace looks down on the place Dauphine and its elegant 17th century architecture, a calm and dignified contrast to the Conciergerie which we shall visit next; the Conciergerie with its grim reminders of the worst horrors of the Revolution, and who knows, still haunted perhaps by the pale ghosts of its hapless victims. For its bare stone cells and gloomy passages were a prelude to the guillotine for the thousands of "aristos" imprisoned here and waiting for death.

Crossing the boulevard and looking back for a general view of this amazing

This beautiful blue and gold clock on the tour de l'Horloge of the Palais de Justice is the work of Germain Pilon, one of the great artists of the French Renaissance.

Tucked away in a corner of the Palais de Justice is the Sainte-Chapelle, created by Saint Louis. Sunlight streaming through its 13th century stained glass windows fill it with light and colour.

Notre-Dame is "not just a building, ▶ *it is a person" (Paul Claudel). Undisputed queen of Paris, she towers above the surrounding buildings of the Ile de la Cité.*

22

complex of buildings, we begin to realise that it represents in one small area a whole microcosm of human activity, while the island itself represents another and larger one. There is the Palace itself opposite us where justice is meted out daily; and alongside us stands the Préfecture de Police on the famous quai des Orfèvres, which even without the help of Maigret has its daily tally of suspects, witnesses and criminals to deal with. Then, there is the Sainte-Chapelle where Mass is still said every day, though plays and concerts are given there too nowadays (as indeed they are also in the Conciergerie).

So, side by side we have the Law and the Police dominating this side of the island, in buildings far less impressive than those across the road which we have already visited. No treasures lie hidden behind the walls here and only the bullet holes left at the Liberation attract any attention. Here are Justice and Police, those interdependent forces, and medicine too.

The Hôtel-Dieu, a major consultant and maternity hospital, has only been on the site for a hundred years or so, but the present buildings are the heirs to a great mediaeval hospital in which yesterday's doctors carried out their work of healing. And even when medicine was powerless in the face of death, help lay close at hand. God, the Saviour, was all around, on the one hand in the Sainte-Chapelle and on the other in Notre-Dame. So here in the space of just a few hundred metres lie all the fundamental bases of civilization.

Notre-Dame! Notre-Dame de Paris! The great cathedral is the heroine of the epic novel by Victor Hugo which in 1831 marked the start of a Gothic revival. Notre-Dame — the centre then of a neo-Gothic or Romantic revival, just as she had been the centre of Gothic life in 12th century Paris. Around her, the whole teeming life, not only of the island, but of the entire city revolved, and throughout the Middle Ages she was the mainspring of all the intellectual and spiritual life of Paris. And here again, it was in the Ile de la Cité that it all began.

Here our symbols begin to intertwine: at the very heart of our original ship, the island in the Seine, itself at the very heart of the city, is Notre-Dame, herself another proud ship, a vessel of faith at the centre of the great capital. And this is in two senses the heart of the capital, for it is from the square in front Notre-Dame that all the distances in France are measured, and on motorways all over the country the road signs give the distance to Paris-Notre-Dame.

Two hundred years of unrelenting labour went into the mammoth task of building her, and it brought to a peak a whole tradition of Gothic architecture whose influence was felt all over Europe. From the triple portals and the great rose-window of the west front, sur-

The stands of the bouquinistes on the quays are survivors of another era — over two hundred of them make up one huge open-air bookshop.

What a pleasure it is to search through the rows of books and old prints displayed in the green boxes which are shut down and padlocked each night.

mounted by two massive square towers, to the bold flying buttresses of the apse, the great church is a masterpiece. Subjected to the inevitable ravages of time — and even more to those of man — the cathedral several times narrowly escaped destruction. By the 19th century it was in a state of utter dilapidation until major restoration work was finally decided upon. Some of that work has been criticized and perhaps the artistic unity of the building has in some respects been impaired, but today, particularly since the great spring-cleaning operation on Paris a few years ago, Notre-Dame is once again gleaming white as she must have been in her early days, and as majestic and awe-inspiring as ever. For after all she guards so many priceless treasures. Apart from the more obvious

ones, the paintings, the sculptures, the stained-glass windows and the saintly relics, there are others, less concrete but no less a part of her, like the sound of the great organ, the long climb up to the grotesque gargoyles on her towers and the breath-taking views of the city and its river spread as far as the eye can see.

Directly below, a splash of green marks the gardens which surround the cathedral at the eastern end, the poop of our ship — the prow is green too — and as we come down from the tower and make our way to the water's edge, we find ourselves confronted by another island only a few yards away across a narrow finger of the Seine. The Ile Saint-Louis, which was originally two smaller islands, beckons across a small footbridge. Its beautiful classical buildings seem invit-

ingly close, but just for the moment we shall resist the temptation to cross over and explore, for we shall return in another chapter to this and perhaps other islands.

Now it is time to disembark from our island ship, for the delights of the mainland await us.

∎

One end of the Ile de la Cité, the ▶ prow of our great ship, is a fisherman's paradise.

The metropolis has not yet swallowed up all the small traders, as this flower-seller and his barrow show.

HAVING DECIDED TO MOVE out from the island, we are immediately faced with a dilemma. Which way do we go! North or south? North to the busy commercial heart of the city, or south along the famous boulevards of the Latin Quarter? For right in the heart of the city lies the great left/right dividing line of the Seine, which for two hundred years or more has reflected the right and left of French politics. This division may at first seem an over-simplification, but to the people of Paris it is a fact of life. It has affected the way the town has developed and the growth of its population. It has become embedded in the life, the customs, in the very fabric of the city. The two banks sit facing one another in silent contradiction, and for every action on the one there is an equal and opposite reaction on the other. This division is very apparent in the attitudes and mentality of the people, and a *rive gauche* label is every bit as descriptive every bit as evocative as the *appellation contrôlée* of a great French wine.

If we go south on to the left bank, we shall be at the centre of the intellectual life of the capital, a focal point to which artists, writers and students have been drawn throughout the centuries. Here, as well as its literary and scholarly associations, everything bears the "left bank" hallmark: the cafés, the shops, the very air one breathes, and above all the people, who are very conscious of the privilege they enjoy. They are "left bank" and proud of it. They show a condescending sympathy for the "other lot", the spiritually poor bourgeoisie on the right bank, whose world is based entirely on money and class. To speak of the "right" is to speak of a limited, materialistic, politically right-wing society, whose sole concerns are business and the prestige it gives. And indeed it does seem to be true that, popular myths aside, this dichotomy has some basis in fact. For on the left bank we find all the publishing houses, most of the avant-garde theatres and galleries, the risqué night-clubs, bookshops of every kind, and those famous cafés where writers and philosophers have met throughout the centuries to argue, to discuss, to exchange ideas.

And so we could go on, for the list of these left bank activities is endless. Its keynote today is youth, everything is fun, every wild extravagance of fashion has

left bank... right bank...

Fremiet's bronze sea-horses amid the fountains of the Observatoire.

its day here and its effervescent life never stops, night or day.

The right bank on the other hand is in complete contrast — a far more serious place altogether. Here are the banks, the insurance companies, the stock exchange, the multi-national firms, the whole business and financial world. Of course there are cafés, theatres and shops, but over here they are more formal, more luxurious, more up-market. Almost ceremonial in their self-importance! This is a world where a tie is *de rigueur* and the great couturiers come into their own. For the right bank is, and has long been, the province of the *beau monde,* grand, elegant, wealthy, perfectly aware of its own position and ever ready to patronize the "intellectuals" across the river, conscious of its own superiority, the very top drawer of Paris society.

So here we have the two distinct faces of Paris, left bank and right bank, with everything on the one reflecting in contradictory terms the life of the other. But let us look first in a little more detail at the left bank which is the hub of the intellectual life of the capital.

As the original settlement of the Parisii grew and spilled over beyond the limits of their island home, it was to the south of the river, along the line of what is now the boulevard Saint-Michel that their Roman conquerors expanded, building all those great municipal edifices that one associates with the towns they colonized. For as we go up either the boulevard itself or the even older rue Saint-Jacques to the top of the hill, we begin to realize that it could not have been mere coincidence which packed so many architectural treasures into such a small space. This whole area is a heritage of Rome. The buildings which stand along these streets have in the course of the centuries replaced many that were originally built by the Romans. The 19th century fontaine Saint-Michel is on the site of an ancient cattle trough, the Sorbonne and the Collège de France are on the sites of the old Roman baths, and the Panthéon like some modern forum stands on that of the ancient Roman one at the top of the hill. Did I say hill? For this is no ordinary hill, and though it is only sixty-five metres above sea level, Paris has the

audacity to call it a mountain! It is the montagne Sainte-Geneviève, so named in honour of the courageous woman who saved Paris from the barbarians in the 5th century and became her patron saint. So this "mountain" is really a metaphorical one, a symbol, of the indomitable spirit of Paris. And the streets which surround it have seen in their day everything from the solemn funeral processions of great national figures winding slowly up to the Panthéon, to the riotous practical jokes played by students of the Sorbonne in their carnival frolics, and children roller-skating or skateboarding in the great amphitheatre of the Arènes de Lutèce.

But let us cross the river again, for throughout the history of Paris this delicate left/right balance has seldom failed to operate. As the left bank grew, so the right bank followed — or vice versa. As early as the Middle Ages, when the establishment of the schools and faculties on the left bank was earning it the name of the Latin Quarter, the right was developing in a contrasting way. The central axis of the city had long run quite naturally along the right bank quays, and as

a result of the city's position and resources, commerce and industry began to appear on this northern bank. Ports were built and canals too; and the first main routes north, which were in time to develop into the rail and motorway networks of today, linked Paris to the growing industrial areas of her northern provinces.

And as early as the 12th century, the *Halles* of Paris were created out of the multitude of earlier street markets in the capital, fulfilling a purpose diametrically opposed to that of the Sorbonne which looked over at them from across the river. There on the left bank the Sorbonne supplied the spiritual and intellectual needs of Paris, while here in the *Halles* on the right bank it was the material needs of the city that were catered for. The enormous market was like a kingdom in itself. And what a chaotic kingdom it was! For almost eight centuries this growing monster of a market daily swallowed up and disgorged the mountains of victuals and provisions of every kind which poured in from the countryside of the Ile-de-France and beyond. It was a violent and insalubrious place and it continued to be so even after it was housed in the 19th century *Halles,* with their lofty glazed roof arcades over a framework of steel and wrought iron. The daily traffic of goods in and out, the garish colours and overpowering market smells, the rough vulgarity of the stallholders and the huge muscular porters — *les forts des Halles* — are powerfully described and brought to life in Zola's famous novel, *Le Ventre de Paris.* But Zola might with equal justification also have represented this *ventre* as a "heart", beating night and day, throbbing and pulsating twenty-four hours out of twenty-four to sustain the life of Paris.

And woven into this pattern of loading and unloading, of shouting and fighting, were the dozens of cafés and restaurants — and the ever-present prostitutes — serving the appetites of all who bought and sold here. It was like some vast theatrical production with a cast of thousands, putting on non-stop performances to satisfy everybody's material and physical needs, played out against an ever-changing backdrop of colour, deafening noise and all-pervading smells.

Now though, the old Halles are no more. The market has been banished to the perimeter of the city, making way for the vast project of the new Beaubourg complex and the ultra-modern and highly controversial architecture of the colourful Pompidou Centre. But we shall come to that later?

Now if we are to follow truly the historical development of the city's boundaries on this, our first venture beyond the confines of its original island, we must widen our horizons to include in the second of these concentric circles which show how Paris was growing, the Louvre, the Saint-Jacques quarter and the place de Grève on the right bank, and the schools and faculties of the Latin Quarter on the left. For it was the circumference of this larger circle which became the second fortified boundary of Paris, built by Philippe-Auguste at the end of the 12th century. "Enceinte 2!" as a film title would put it today! The circle grew in more or less equal proportions on both sides of the river and the dichotomy was still there. It was still left against right, spiritual against material, trade against learning. But student and tradesman, mob and bourgeoisie, all became fused together in some mysterious chemical formula to produce... Paris! Fortunately, the resultant mixture was a stable one which has withstood the test of time. We are reminded once again of that popular song: *Paris sera toujours Paris!*

■

e dome of the Panthéon seen ›ond the Luxembourg gardens ich are a favourite retreat for the dents of all nationalities who ck here diving the summer. (PRE-)ING PAGE.)

Rive gauche... at the bottom of the Boul'Mich is all the animation and lively vivacity of the place Saint-André-des-Arts, at the hub of the Latin Quarter.

Rive droite... the formal luxury of the Ritz Hotel in the elegant place Vendôme where Proust and Fitzgerald used to dine. The Ritz was the first hotel in Paris to install private bathrooms in all its rooms.

The Ministry of Justice, place Vendôme, seen reflected in the windows of one of the great Paris shirt-makers. ▶

SADLY, IN THE COURSE OF THIS CENTURY, scientific and technological progress has slowly but surely dehumanized our society. One sign among many of this trend is the way names are continually being replaced by numbers. Instead of the long familiar BAGatelle and PIGalle phone numbers, we now have the anonymous 224s and 744s in their place, and the voice of the girl at the telephone exchange has gone for ever. In just the same way the buses have jetisoned their old destination boards, along with the human face of the conductor standing on his platform. They all now bear an anonymous number: 68 or 72 or 84... Gone are the former AE, BD and AX lines, gone even the simple way of naming the bus after its point of departure and its destination – Madeleine-Bastille...

But we are going to recreate just such a line and call it Louvre-Concorde. Imaginary it may be, but nevertheless it is essential to the journey we are going to make today. This is far and away the most popular tourist route in Paris, straight as a die, rich in aesthetically pleasing perspectives. Here the tourist is king! Everywhere car parks and traffic lanes are reserved for the modern double-decker coaches which, with their bilingual guides and somewhat blasé drivers, have long been a familiar feature of the Paris landscape.

The route we are going to follow is a triumphant example of the use of the straight line in architectural planning, and here we are dealing with not one but three parallel and equally straight axes. The main axis starts at the heart of the original palace of the Louvre and

runs through the Tuileries gardens to the place de la Concorde. On either side of it there are parallel axes, reflections almost, all of which reveal an enormous variety of architectural and other treasures. To the left runs the Seine with its quays, its line of balustrades and glimpses of the great buildings on the other side of the river. On the right there is the long rue de Rivoli with its famous arcades and long row of balconies, and parallel again, the rue Saint-Honoré, narrow but full of attractive little squares and interesting churches.

Whichever of these parallel paths we take, we shall emerge in the incomparable place de la Concorde, the political heart of France, midway between the Assemblée Nationale and the Élysée Palace, both of which we can see from here. A few short steps will take us into

Louvre-Concorde: a paradise for tourists

Hidden away among the greenery of the Tuileries gardens, Barye's lion has been tamed by the children who love to clamber over it.

the most famous avenue in the world, the Champs-Élysées, at the top of which rises the imposing outline of the Arc de Triomphe to close the magnificent perspective that was opened up for us way back in the heart of the Louvre.

This then is the area we are going to explore today, so let us now go back to our starting point, the Louvre, and have a closer and more systematic look at all the treasures we have so far merely glanced at along our route. But first, before we enter the Louvre itself, we must just take a quick look over our shoulder, for, tucked away among the big

◄ *The Cour Carrée at the heart of the original palace of the Louvre with its beautifully decorated facades.*

A "Son et Lumière" performance in the Cour Carrée on a summer evening.

A dramatic photograph of one of Maillol's great nude statues in the Carrousel gardens between the two wings of the Louvre.

The celebrated Venus of Milo discovered in the ruins of Mêlos in 1830 and installed in the Louvre museum.

The Second Empire facade of the Louvre seen from the pont des Arts.

department stores is a church which we must on no account miss. This is Saint-Germain-l'Auxerrois, and if we brave the traffic and cross over the road to look at it more closely we shall be well rewarded for our trouble. This church not only offers one of the best examples in Paris of flamboyant Gothic and the transition to Renaissance architecture, but it is also redolent with history. For it was once the Royal church, the church of the Louvre. It was here that the signal for the horrendous massacre of Saint Bartholomew was given, here that the tocsin was sounded in the days of the Commune, and here that Molière was married.

As we turn away from the church and wait to cross the road again, the jostling crowds, the clamour, the streams of cars, all the turbulence of modern life, pale into insignificance, for there, standing in all its magnificence before us is the Louvre. The Louvre, this palace of the kings of France on which each of them has left his mark! The Louvre, whose continuity of design was preserved throughout the centuries as palace after

palace was added to it! The Louvre, where there is so much for us to see! The palace was originally a fortress, built by Philippe-Auguste on what was the eastern boundary of Paris. Comparatively recent alterations have lowered the level of the ground in front of its façades by excavating broad, deep trenches which go right down to the 17th century foundations. This has added seven metres to the height of the walls and the fortress's original dimensions are now revealed. The sheer perfection of the present day Louvre is universally acknowledged, and though some parts of the buildings crumbled away during times of neglect in the past, what a great treasure house it is!

It is all perfect: the great Colonnade leading into the square courtyard (the Cour Carrée), its splendid facades and pavilions, the lofty archways of the original entrances (the "Guichets") — all planned in a perfect "U" shape, with the original palace at the base of the "U" and the divergent wings of the newer palaces stretching out on either side into

the gardens. The architectural coherence of all these buildings, which were conceived and built over such a long period of time, is amazing. For despite the varying styles of the architects and artists who worked on it over the centuries, the palace is a happy marriage of many different styles, Renaissance, Louis XIV, 18th century and Napoleonic. Even the Second Empire additions do not look out of place, for none of the artists ever tried to shock or to destroy the work of his predecessors. Each sought instead to harmonize his work with theirs, to supplement the beauty of the whole.

So today, despite the traffic roaring continuously past outside, despite the coaches and the thousands of tourists they bring, and the daily to-ing and fro-ing of all the government officials going about their business, we have only to cross the Cour Carrée and step out into the base of that "U" to find ourselves in an entirely different world as we look out between the two great wings of the palace. For stretched out before us, in a setting created by architects and planners over three centuries or more, is that unique avenue stretching away to the horizon. The Tuileries Palace which used to block the view was burned to the ground during the Commune riots, and since 1871 there has been nothing to interrupt the long unbroken line from the Louvre right up to the Étoile. Straight and true, Napoleon's "Voie Triomphale" runs ahead of us, like the shining blade of a beautiful sword which, after cutting three lovely gardens into the heart of the palace, swings upward as if in triumph to become the Obelisk in the place de la Concorde. And we can carry our simile further and liken the Carrousel arch through which our sword-blade passes, to the pummel encircling its hilt, while finally, another blade's length away, its dazzling point is embedded in the heart of the massive Arc de Triomphe.

Now let us come back to earth and have a closer look at the Carrousel arch itself and read the story of Napoleon's

The "guichets", the original entrances to the Louvre which allow cars through to the place du Carrousel.

The bust of Molière in the foyer of the Comédie Française which adjoins the Palais-Royal.

The Palais-Royal, a magnificent example of 18th century architecture and one of the most fashionable rendez-vous in Paris in its time.

triumphs in Europe which are recorded in the series of bas-reliefs between its lovely columns of roseate marble. And passing through the arch we find ourselves in one of the most beautiful gardens in the whole of Paris, with its fountains and flowerbeds and pavilions. Maillol's great bronze nudes planted here and there around the lawns and flowerbeds turn the wide open spaces of the gardens into a huge open-air museum. The only other parks in Paris which invite comparison are the esplanade des Invalides across the river, and the long sweeps of avenues out at Versailles — and all three date from that same classical period when great buildings and their parks and the avenues through them were planned together as a harmoniously integrated whole.

We reach now the end of the gardens and suddenly we can see where all these parallel lines — the quays, the gardens, the tree-lined streets — have been leading us. They all finally take us into the beautiful place de la Concorde, with its ancient Obelisk, its great bronzes and statues and its fountains lit up at night by those lovely old-fashioned street lamps of which Paris seems to have preserved so many. And in front of us, like a mirror reflection of the gardens we have just come through, the Champs-Élysées are beckoning to us from the other side of the place.

Anyway it would be a mistake to let our admiration for the perfect perspectives of this central axis which we have been following, blind us to the beauties on both sides of it. The Seine, for one! Of course there are always lovely reflections in the water, reflections of patient fishermen by the water's edge, of the heavy iron mooring-rings on the quaysides, of pairs of lovers drifting by, of overhanging trees. But here on the quai des Tuileries and the quai du Louvre we have the splendour of the riverside facades of the palaces as well, and all the charm of quiet paths between the trees along the bank and the gardens themselves.

But it is on the other side of the Louvre, along the parallel rue de Rivoli

The Carrousel arch, seen there wi the Louvre in the background, co memorates Napoleon's victories Europe.

and rue Saint-Honoré that we shall discover the last, but by no means the least, of the treasures this *1er arrondissement* has to offer.   Across the rue de Rivoli, at right-angles to the Louvre, there are the colonnades, gardens and elegant buildings of the Palais-Royal.   And though today the solemn halls of the Conseil d'État and the Ministry of Culture have replaced the delightful frivolity of the rakish 18th century, and the palace itself is out of bounds to the public, we can

The window of one of the great jewellers' shops in the place Vendôme.

Two views of the rue de Rivoli with its fine 19th century buildings and arcades as it runs parallel to the Tuileries gardens into the place de la Concorde.

explore the shops and little cafés under the arcades round the perimeter of the gardens, or better still, stroll through the enchanting gardens themselves, where nothing disturbs the birds in their singing, or the quivering fountains and swaying trees.   Even the sound of the park-keeper's mowing-machine seems somehow idyllic in this peaceful setting.   What a joy it must be to live or work in these delightful surroundings, to have the freedom of those elegant balconies and terraces!   But we ordinary mortals must be content to look enviously on, and perhaps wander through the arcades near the entrance to the Palais and have a look at the Comédie Française.

Or we might prefer just to sit here and dream of the poetry of days gone by, of the Paris which so many Parisian writers from Colette to Léon-Paul Fargue have succeeded in evoking so delicately and yet so powerfully.

Now into the rue de Rivoli and its imposing 19th century facades, and the rue Saint-Honoré with its older 18th cen-

tury buildings! As we stroll along here we shall risk cricking our necks if we are not careful, for there are so many tantalizing things to see on all sides of us — glimpses of the Louvre on our left, and on our right many a little church we ought to have a look at. There is the little Bohemian community of artists in the parish of Saint-Roch. Concerts are often given in the church, whose walls still bear the scars of the royalist insurrection of Vendémiaire which was put down somewhat ruthlessly by a certain lieutenant Bonaparte...

And finally, to finish our exploration of the *1er arrondissement* we find one last architectural gem — the place Vendôme. There is something rather appropriate in describing it as a "gem" for all the famous jewellers have their premises here alongside the Ritz and the Ministry of Justice. The square is surrounded by impressive early 19th century houses whose lofty facades are decorated with ornate wrought-ironwork and gilding. And, believe it or not, the square is closed from time to time when sump-

tuous receptions are being held in one or another of its great houses, and then, flood-lit and red-carpeted, this most elegant of all the squares in Paris displays to the full its former royal splendour. ■

The place Vendôme, built at the end of Louis XIV's reign. The central column, in honour of Napoleon was originally encased in the bronze of over a thousand cannons captured at the battle of Austerlitz.

Fountains of the Tuileries gardens. ▶

LEAVING THE SPLENDOUR of the *1er arrondissement* behind us, let us move back into that fascinating circular geometry which underlies the basic pattern of the capital. At this point we must begin to study the city as a tree-surgeon would observe the growth-ings of an ancient oak or cedar. Gradually widening our field of investigation from ring to ring, we shall endeavour to follow the numerical sequence in our exploration of the various districts. Our only guide will be the huge natural spiral of the twenty *arrondissements,* coiled into a double, sometimes triple-layered sandwich of life as we move from the banks of the Seine to the heights of Ménilmontant, from Châtelet to Nation and maybe even beyond.

Alternating between the meanderings of the Seine and the open green spaces, we could follow this ever-widening spiral through the growing rings of the city to its boundary — the *boulevards extérieurs,* the *boulevard périphérique* and a third, still under construction. But for the moment let us content ourselves with a detailed look at the next three *arrondissements* along our spiral. In its time the great city, in itself a kind of "city centre" for the whole nation has known several successive centres, at a few of which we have already looked. At first there was the original island in the Seine, then the settlements on its banks, then the area round the Louvre — and now here is yet another *centre-ville.* But the pattern of our growing spiral is still

there, for this next group of *arrondissements,* the *2e, 3e,* and *4e,* with which we are going to continue our visit, has grown up within a circle of boulevards. Yes, another ring of boulevards, the earliest and the most famous of all — the *Grands Boulevards,* so dear to Yves Montand, which are a living witness to the everyday life of Paris in the last century. Still part of the pattern, they trace another circle round the ramparts built by Charles V in the 14th century and enlarged by Louis XIII in the 17th. So the city — just as a tree does — lets us read its age by the growing number of its concentric rings — stone rings in this case.

But if this part of the city seems to be its real centre, it is because of its important centres of activity, its chequerboard

the city centre

In the Marais during the Festival. The restaurants of its old buildings brought with it an increase in cultural activity — cafés-théâtres, concerts and open-air entertainments like this...

44 pattern of streets, its self-contained islets of everyday life, its monuments — all combine and unfold before us like a roll of interesting urban cloth. We can cut into it where we will, as a particular need or the whim of the moment dictates. But we shall be all the time conscious of its predominant colours — the natural greys and whites and honey colours of the buildings and the dazzling blues of the sky,

an ever-present contrast in this incomparable city.

We shall begin with the place des Victoires. We have not quite left the *1er arrondissement* for we are only just crossing over into the *2e*. A quick glance over our shoulder still shows us the railings and arcades of the rue de Rivoli and a corner of the Louvre, and we can just make out the gardens of the Palais-

Royal through an opening in yet another series of identical arcades. The whole city lies around us under the blue Paris sky.

Here in the place des Victoires, the thing which strikes us most is the complete harmony between the successive lines of the terrace on which the equestrian statue of the Sun King stands, the road itself curving round it, and the architecturally perfect circle of buildings on the circumference with their splendid uniform facades. The place des Victoires is undoubtedly the most perfect of the many circular *places* you will find tucked away in many a corner of Paris.

More recently, broad avenues have opened up the view until they too disappear into the little streets around the *place,* picturesque because they are narrow and full of small shops and businesses, and because of their delightful names like Petits-Pères and Petits-Champs — and less charming but even more evocative, Vide-Gousset and Chabanais. Make no mistake though! These are not at all the "picturesque little streets" of mediaeval Paris, for they are really an extension of the classical architecture of the place itself, and their rows of tall, austere buildings are disposed in just as disciplined an order as any geometrically formal French garden. Except that here we have streets instead of garden paths and buildings instead of clumps of trees. As for the rest of this "park", we shall find nothing else really outstanding until we reach its outer edge for there, one at each end, stand two really impressive monuments. At one

The hôtel de Sens in the Marais... Its defensive turrets recall the difficult times of the 15th century.

The quayside facades of the Marais' 18th century hôtels.

nd we have the classical Bibliothèque Nationale, that huge reservoir of academic culture, and at the other end, built in the style of a Greco-Roman temple, the Bourse or Stock Exchange, the nerve centre of the city's economic life.

On the eastern edge of the *2ͤ* and right across the *3ͤ arrondissement* there is a great feeling of unity. Once we have crossed the "Sébasto" (the boulevard Sébastopol) into the hundreds of busy streets leading to the former Halles, we are in the Sentier district, a predominantly artisan quarter. The "Arts et Métiers" is here at the top of the rue Beaubourg, and further down is the drapers' and haberdashers' corner of Paris where everything connected with the dressmaking trade can be bought. The main business is wholesale, but if you smile at

them nicely they are not averse to doing a bit of retail trade. Then, as we move on down the rue des Rosiers, past the Temple, we are crossing into the *4ͤ arrondissement,* the old Jewish quarter. A quick look at the map here will show a series of little splashes of green each representing a pleasant green tree-lined square, which one is surprised somehow to find in this human anthill. Anthill, because of all the little corner shops and tiny businesses, human because of the coherence and harmony with which new buildings, houses and public buildings alike, blend in with the old ones along its streets, fusing together the work of many centuries in the continuity of stone.

It is here, moreover, that we find one of the most beautiful collections of buildings that the city has to offer — the

Marais. This quarter, astride the *3ͤ* and the *4ͤ arrondissements,* was one of the main targets of the scheme to restore and protect France's national heritage launched by Malraux around the sixty years. This scheme provided funds to save run-down and in some cases ruined buildings, to protect historic areas from an invasion of incongruous modern development, peel off layers of hideous

Another masterpiece in the Marais: ▶ *the place des Vosges, originally the place Royale designed by Henri IV, is surrounded by a square of identical mansions whose brick and slate are typical of early 17th century architecture.*

The hôtel Carnavalet, for eighteen years the home of Madame de Sévigné, now the historical museum of the city of Paris and one of the loveliest buildings in Paris. Here we see its inner courtyard decorated by Lescot.

stucco from beautiful old facades, replan parks and gardens, restore churches, and in general try to recreate the original atmosphere of an area. Unfortunately in some cases the resultant excess of zeal it inspired produced a rash of exposed beams, pebble-dashed walls and phoney décor which the current "snobisme" insisted were the acme of interior decoration; and as for the outsides of buildings, the over-aesthetic pretensions of the planners left parts of the district looking a bit like an open-air museum. This tendency was aggravated by the enormous jump in property prices and not helped by the fashion for imitation antiques and cheap reproductions which flooded the market and were, alas, considered very "chic" and "très snob" by the undiscerning. But this is perhaps a petty quibble. On the whole the scheme was undoubtedly successful and the Marais area has been saved, as a stroll through its streets and squares will clearly show.

For everything here is beautiful — and the constant reminders of the past at every corner more than make up for the occasionally brash newness which the restorers have sometimes left behind them. For here in the Marais, princely residences and the homes of the great are thick on the ground, built on classically simple lines and surrounded by some more modest buildings among which they stand out, not so much by their greater size as by the magnificent decoration of their facades: the detail of a doorway, a piece of sculpture here, a bas-relief there, and everywhere those lovely balustrades and coats-of-arms. Their courtyards too, as grand as those of many a palace, are full of pillars, arches, balconies and wrought-iron staircases, to say nothing of their

Between Beaubourg and the Halles the picturesque rue Quincampoix, restored to the elegance it had in the 18th century when it was the centre of Law's financial dealing, dealings which resulted in the notorious South Sea Bubble disaster.

A wide-angle lens shows the p. des Vosges with sunlight filte. through the trees and some the thirty-eight beautiful mans. which surround it.

gardens. Many of these splendid *hôtels particuliers*, the town houses of old aristocratic families — Sully, Soubise, Rohan-Strasbourg, Salé, Lamoignon and so on — have been taken over either by the state or by the city of Paris and are now nearly all museums or cultural centres of some kind. And there are many others too, the *hôtels* of Montmort, Tallard, Hérouët, de Marle, Guénégaud, and above all, Carnavalet, now the historical museum of the city of Paris. Then there is the superb hôtel des Ambassadeurs de Hollande, whose facade is perhaps the most beautiful in the whole of the Marais. Beaumarchais lived here for eleven years, and Mozart stayed at the hôtel Beauvais for a few months on his first visit to Paris at the age of seven.

As we stroll slowly from street to street, passing a few churches which make a change in the architectural scene, we shall reach the place des Vosges through its lofty entrance arches. This royal square — it was actually called the place Royale before the Revolutionary council decided to honour the Vosges for their loyalty in paying their taxes promptly — is practically the only surviving example of pre-classical architecture. By its sheer beauty and by the influence it exerted on later periods, it has come to be regarded as an aesthetic showpiece, for it is indeed unique. For one thing, it was the first *place* in Paris to be built round a square, a completely new conception. Previously they had all been round (like the place des Victoires where we started today's journey). Here in the place des Vosges, geometrically square gardens planted with lime-trees are surrounded by another square of about forty incomparable houses. All built in the same style (early 17th cen-

tury) their alternating vertical lines of red brick and honey-coloured stone create a remarkably well-balanced feeling of proportion, from the arcades at street level with the tall slender windows above them, up through the body of the building to the slate roofs which date these masterpieces so precisely.

Madame de Sévigné was born here, Marion de Lorme lived here and so did

Victor Hugo. At the time it was built and again throughout the Romantic period this square was the height of fashion. And so it is again today. In spite of the inevitable art galleries and restaurants which you find here as everywhere else in Paris, the main impression is one of provincial calm, magically preserved as if by an invisible plate-glass window which allows this unique square to go on

Any visit to the Marais must include a glimpse of the lovely courtyards beyond the massive entrance gateways.

49

living at its own serene pace, undisturbed by the world outside and the passage of time.

But we are getting near the limits of this section of Paris, which are those of the arrondissement as well. We shall soon be down by the Seine, but on our way we shall pass one or two of the remaining treasures this quarter has to offer: a fragment of Philippe-Auguste's original wall; two more *hôtels,* those of Sens and Aumont, the last on our route; a pleasant jumble of little streets awaiting the restorer's hand; and alongside the church of Saint-Gervais with its incredible mixture of architectural styles, we shall see what is probably the most beautiful terrace of private houses in the whole of Paris. A raised facade runs above a wide flight of stone steps, in perfect parallel harmony. There is very little decoration, just enough to emphasize the purity of the design. One of the houses was that of the Couperin family of musicians, (Louis Couperin was organist at Saint-Gervais) and each balcony bears the unusual design of an elm tree standing in front of a church.

And then, taking a last stride over those two incongruous neighbours, the Bazar de l'Hôtel de Ville, a big department store, and the Hôtel de Ville, the town hall itself, we find ourselves once again in a *centre-ville* atmosphere with all its familiar characteristics: centuries of building and craftsmanship, the tour Saint-Jacques, the Châtelet fountain, the theatres — and the crowds, the commerce, the traffic, all crammed into this tiny area at the end of the long roads from the north which daily discharge their overflow of men and materials from the surrounding suburbs.

Then, from the midst of this swarming hive of activity there sprang — the Monster — the Pompidou Centre, that huge mass of brightly coloured metal. Emerging like some futuristic dinosaur from the mediaeval surroundings of former brothels in dubious streets, it has aroused contradictory passions since the

◀ *Like a great ocean liner, the Pompidou Centre has outside gangways which take the public up level with the rooftops of the buildings among which it is anchored.*

The gargoyles of Notre-Dame look down in amazement at the Centre Pompidou which has revolutionized the old Halles district.

beginning of its existence in 1977. Opinions have varied between a violently indignant refusal to accept this savage intrusion, and fervent enthusiasm for this bold leap into the contemporary. But, despite the mocking letters addressed to the "factory" or the "plumber", the reality of the situation is shown by the record-breaking attendance figures. Far more people visit the Pompidou Centre each year than go to Versailles, the Louvre or even the Eiffel Tower! So the original aim of the centre, to bring art and culture to the mass of the people has been more than fulfilled; for in spite of the controversial appearance of the building, it represents a serious endeavour to democratize culture.

In addition, it has revitalized the quarter after the departure of the Halles to the outer suburbs — and nobody seems to be complaining about that!

So, despite the inevitable teething troubles and problems of adjustment, the Centre today is like one of the great meeting-places of ancient times, and the concourse in front of it, an open space where all and sundry are at liberty to express themselves in every conceivable art-form. Long may we be able to find here everything from anonymous singers and unknown folk groups to dramatically exhibitionist fire-eaters and sword-swallowers! ∎

The funnels on the edges of the square continue the nautical image, and a crowd of passengers is always on deck to applaud the varied entertainments offered.

The underground Forum which replaced the Baltard metal arcades. Saint-Eustache is in the background left.

Crowds milling round the strange ▶ objects encountered from time to time at Beaubourg, alias the Pompidou Centre, to encourage a sense of adventure and discovery. Record-breaking attendance figures prove the success of the venture.

IT RUNS FROM THE SEINE back again to the Seine, across the full length of the three riverside *arrondissements,* but curving slightly away from the river to form the southern half of a long oval, the top half of which is made up of the *arrondissements* on the opposite bank which we have already met.

"It" is the boulevard Saint-Germain which runs from the Ile Saint-Louis at one end to Concorde at the other. Today, the oneway traffic along the great boulevard flows up from the Concorde end, so it is there that we must start our journey. And if this and the boulevard Saint-Michel are the twin jewels in this left bank crown, is it not fitting that they should meet as they do to form a symbolic cross? Fitting too that we should start

out near the home of the Assemblée Nationale and the nearby Ministry of Foreign Affairs, two imposing edifices which remind us that some of the upper echelons of society with all their wealth and tradition, reside on this side of the water too. For the faubourg Saint-Germain is to the left bank what the faubourg Saint-Honoré is to the right. Both comprise basically the same big houses with their wide *portes-cochères,* built to admit the fine horse-carriages of the last century. They overlook this section of the boulevard in an unbroken line, set back a little from the road, sheltered by the great trees which are a feature of all these lovely avenues.

Many of the great mansions house government ministries or foreign embassies both here on the boulevard and in

the network of streets which run either parallel or at right angles to it: Grenelle, Varenne, de l'Université, Verneuil, and a few others which make up the heart of the diplomatic quarter.

In this enclave of today's elite, republican as it is, we feel we should like to open up every one of these great houses and go inside, just to see the sheer, often monumental size of it all, to appreciate the fine luxurious furnishings under the richly moulded ceilings, and to gaze in admiration at the gardens, which re-echo the grandeur of the facades in the parallel lines of their quiet green avenues. The buildings belonging to the state always have the gate into the courtyard left open. So if you crane your neck past the inevitable gendarme on duty, you can just catch a glimpse of at least part of

the faubourg Saint-Germain

*Antique shops line the streets of
the faubourg Saint-Germain.*

the interior. But the gardens are a different matter altogether! To see most of them you have to get an official invitation — or fly over by helicopter, which in any case would be illegal! Admittedly a former Prime Minister ordered the removal of the solid panels from the railings at the back of the Hôtel Matignon — his official residence — and the public can now admire from the far end of the magnificent gardens its trees and flowerbeds and the green of its lawns which stretch for well over three hundred metres.

Really though, we ought to explore the boulevard Saint-Germain on foot, so that we could start from the other end, at number one, and work down. Then we should discover the real rive gauche in the *5ᵉ* and *6ᵉ arrondissements* before the boulevard moves up the social ladder into these "posh" districts. Here in the streets behind the main thoroughfare we are in the friendly, light-hearted world of the Latin Quarter, surrounded by the crowds of *lycéens* and students who fill the streets and congregate in their Bohemian cafés to talk and argue and play their ubiquitous guitars. The working people of the neighbourhood, the shop-assistants and smart little secretaries are here too as they always have been, and even if the Science Faculty has taken over the Halle aux Vins, the little markets and shops are still there, all contributing to

the incredible hubbub which reaches its peak as we join the famous boulevard Saint-Michel, the incomparable "Boul'Mich".

We could, as we set out from the Ile Saint-Louis at the end of the boulevard Saint-Germain have made a detour along the quai Saint-Bernard to visit the Jardin des Plantes, with its natural history museum and its zoo, to watch the children rushing around looking at cages of mischievous monkeys or rather tired-looking lions. Then we could have taken a different route down to the Boul'Mich, passing on our way the beautiful Paris mosque and the Institut Musulman — frequented by mere infidels for its Turkish baths and mint tea! Next follows a series of tiny, picturesque old districts, all better known by familiar abbreviations than by their full names. "La Maub" for example is Maubert-Mutualité. Mitterrand lives there — Pompidou used to live just opposite on the Ile Saint-Louis — and the daily tumult rises to fever pitch on evenings when there are political meetings in the hall of the "Mutu". A bit further on and it is the "Mouff", alias the rue Mouffetard, where the whole street is one long market — one of those markets where produce of every kind is thrown haphazardly on to stalls, often almost on to the pavement, and the strident Parisian voices of its stall-holders rival those of the fishwives

On the left bank between the Seine and the Panthéon: a "bougnat" weighing up coal for his customers.

The shops and stalls of the ⸢ Mouffetard which is one lc street market.

Surprisingly this wild garden is right in the heart of the city — in a corner of the Muséum National d'Histoire Naturelle.

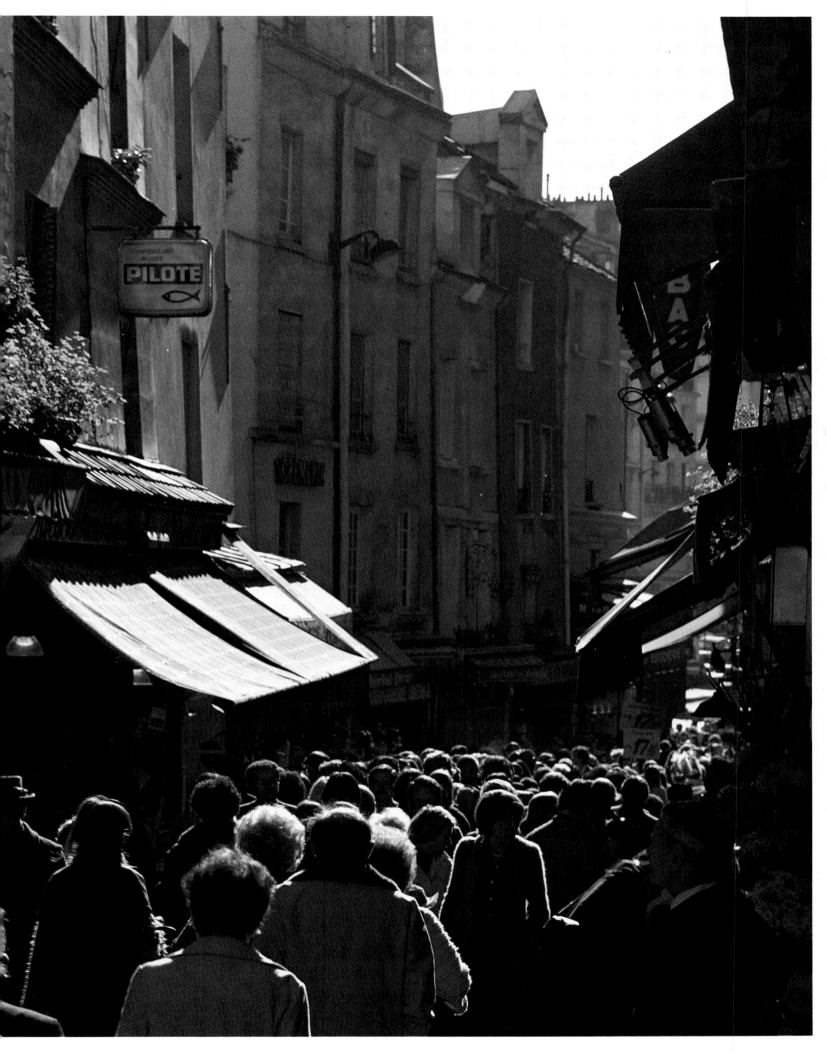

The Bibliothèque Sainte-Geneviève whose lofty metal pillars give the impression of a church.

of Marseilles as they shout to advertise their wares.

Still among the schools and colleges, we come to the streets which make up the "Contrescarpe", with their evocative names like Épée-de-Bois, Puits-de-l'Hermite, Ortolan, Pot-de-Fer, Estrapade. And the transition to the Boul'Mich is quite a natural one for it is at the same time both the frontier and the heart of this Latin Quarter where students (bona fide ones or not), tourists and the local people are constantly rubbing shoulders.

We must not forget the rue Saint-Jacques either. It may appear at first sight to be just a pale reflection of the Boul'Mich, a faithful companion on their joint way up to the Luxembourg, but it is actually the oldest street in Paris. Splendid monuments and churches blossomed all along these two parallel thoroughfares and in the streets and squares round about. The old monuments have become the schools, colleges and libraries of today, but most of the churches are still in use — from Saint-Séve-

The baroque dome of the Val-de-Grâce, rivalling that of the Panthéon, surmounts the church of this military hospital which dates from the 17th century and is still in use.

The tiny church of Saint-Julien-le-Pauvre and its square, photographed in winter.

rin at the bottom of the Boul'Mich, to Saint-Étienne-du-Mont at the top of the hill. Cafés, restaurants and bookshops, rendez-vous for students and scholars alike also flourish here. They are to be found every few yards or so, from the place Saint-Michel at the bottom — a favourite haunt of motor-bike maniacs and connaisseurs of exotic foods — right up to the trees and fountains of the Luxembourg gardens (the "Luco") at the top.

The Boul'Mich does go further, but its atmosphere changes and it takes on an air of middle-class refinement by the time it — and its still parallel twin, the rue Saint-Jacques — reaches the Val-de-Grâce, a military hospital endowed with a superb church whose Baroque dome rivals in grandeur that of the neo-classical Pantheon. This new feeling of calm reaches across the road, though the *arrondissement* does not, for the line of the boulevard marks the boundary with the 6ᵉ where we still find the same desirable blocks of flats, with an added bonus here — an unimpaired view of the Luxem-

bourg Gardens. And, what is more, there is another garden close by, far smaller, but just as charming to those lucky enough to live in the vicinity, the tiny Jardin de l'Observatoire. From Carpeaux's famous bronze sculpture at its gate, there is an uninterrupted view over the clear open spaces of the Luxembourg gardens right to Marie de Medici's palace, the seat of the modern Senate.

And the lovers, and the students — book in hand — who occupy the park benches, the children playing with their boats on the peaceful waters of the round pond, serve to make us all the more aware of the utter tranquillity of this vast oasis of green calm, with its terraces and balustrades half hidden among the trees.

Beyond the park gates, which stay open till nightfall, lies another world. Among its busy shopping streets and rather ordinary buildings, the pillared facade of the Odéon theatre stands out. After a chequered existence, the theatre's fortunes were restored when the actor-manager Gémier took over its direction and stars of the calibre of Jean-Louis

Barrault appeared on its stage. Another landmark is the church of Saint-Sulpice with its oddly asymetrical towers, in a neighbourhood which was formerly noted for the ostentatious piety of its residents, until it was colonized by the great couturier houses and then, its character changed.

Now we are getting on towards Montparnasse and already there is more movement in the air, more heavy traffic coming in. For we are at the dividing line between the city centre and the suburbs beyond the circle of the *grands boulevards*. But instead of staying to explore Montparnasse, we shall head back towards Saint-Germain, for it is there, between the Vieux-Colombier theatre and the Seine that the real heart of the faubourg lies, in the streets around the beautiful romanesque church which has given the whole district the unquenchable source of its fame, its raison d'être, its very name: Saint-Germain-des-Prés.

Sandwiched between the Bohemian 5ᵉ and the elegant 7ᵉ *arrondissements*, the

The church of Saint-Séverin, full of architectural jewels dating from the 13th to the 16th centuries.

60 faubourg has an atmosphere all its own which we shall find nowhere else in Paris. Hidden away among its old streets is the tiny place Furstenberg, the globes of its old street-lamps shining on the studio where Delacroix painted. Cheerful, jostling crowds fill the pavements by day, and the roads too are taken over at night by pedestrians out for a stroll and artists trying to sell their usually naïve paintings. Bric-à-brac is displayed for sale on the ground under the trees and mechanical singing-birds perch on the church railings — all for sale. And every terrace and bar is crowded with people who have come to see, and more importantly to be seen, in the faubourg Saint-Germain.

This crossroad in the heart of the left bank, where the existentialism of Sartre

One of the many statues in the Luxembourg gardens,

and children sailing their boats on the round pond in front of the old palace of Marie de Medici which is now the seat of the French Senate.

and Boris Vian spilled over into every bistro on the square and every smoke-filled basement room, has entered into the realms of legend. The very names of the cafés they frequented are branded on the memory like passwords to some superior existentialist world: Lipp, Café de Flore, les Deux Magots! Every morning the waiters, dressed in the traditional white apron, perform the ritual arrangement of the tables and chairs outside on the terraces. At the unearthly hour at which this ritual takes place, only the most dedicated could appreciate the unique flavour of the first cup of coffee of the day as he watches the newly-risen sun playing on the old tower of Saint-Germain-des-Prés.

Other equally ancient streets lead us down to the river. Every corner seems to be full of memories, to hide some little evidence of past adventures. So we come to the prestigious buildings which line the quay. The Louvre is just a short distance away across the water and beside us stand the 18th century Monnaie (the Mint), the Institut de France and the Bibliothèque Mazarine, both 17th century buildings, the latter standing on the exact site of the famous Tour de Nesle, and finally the 19th century École des Beaux-Arts, with its beautiful collection of Renaissance fragments in the courtyard. Now the 7e arrondissement is not far away and its influence can already be felt. From the rue de Seine to the rue Bonaparte and the rue des Saints-Pères, it is nothing but art galleries antique shops, each one striving to be the most elegant — and probably the most expensive! Fortunately it costs nothing to window-shop, so although we may have to crane our necks on the narrow pavements to see the decoration on the upper storeys of the old houses, it is well worth the effort. For this is an art exhibition *par excellence* and it is absolutely free, for the benefit of passersby and the odd driver caught in one of the interminable traffic jams.

The 7e arrondissement does not end here, nor even at the junction of the boulevard Saint-Germain and the quai

Saint-Germain-des-Prés, the olde church in Paris, presides over t. Café des Deux-Magots...

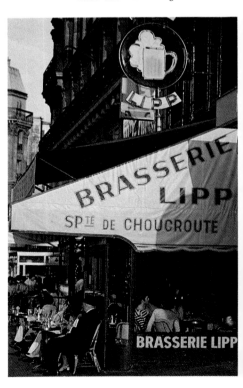

The Medici fountain with its statue of Polyphemus and Diana half-hidden by the overhanging trees.

... and the Brasserie Lipp, two famous cafés where philosophers and writers have long met.

d'Orsay; but even so, as we cross the boulevard des Invalides and in so doing leave the faubourg behind, new vistas open up before our eyes. The atmosphere changes once again and a little further on nearer the river we find ourselves in the lively yet elegant parish of Saint-Pierre-du-Gros-Caillou. There is an air of solid prosperity in the luxury blocks of flats lined up along broad, airy avenues which you might mistake for private drives until you realize that they are right on the Champ-de-Mars, the vast park where the *14 juillet* was first commemorated and which has been permanently open to the public ever since.

But even opulence like this pales into insignificance beside the twin wonders which frame it, for this "other" *7ᵉ arrondissement* opens with a view of the Invalides and closes with one of the Eiffel Tower.

On the boundary between the *7ᵉ* and *15ᵉ arrondissements*, there is a lovely square which commands one of the most impressive views in Paris. To stand here is like standing on the hinge of a pair of geometric compasses, so accurately spaced apart are the dome of the Invalides, seen on the right, and the courtyard of the École Militaire on the left. A short stroll down to the quay will reveal impressive views of the two great esplanades which lead down to the Seine. The first is the wide open rectangle of the Esplanade des Invalides; the other, the Champ-de-Mars in front of the École Militaire. Then, if we turn to look across the river, we shall see the twin palaces of the right bank, the Grand Palais and the Petit Palais whose sculpted horses and glass roofs dominate the horizon; finally there is the Palais de Chaillot, whose monumentally austere lines have replaced the horrible pink stucco of the old Trocadero.

In this part of the city though, everything is eclipsed by the Eiffel Tower, the "old lady" as Paris has come to call her. Three hundred and twenty metres high, composed of 15,000 solid metal struts and two and a half million rivets, it is still one of the most popular tourist attractions in Paris. They flock to see the views over the city and beyond, for from any of its upper platforms the hills of the Ile-de-France are often visible. The Eiffel Tower is Paris, as the numbers of tourists prove. We have only to look at the multitude of postcards — one almost expects them to be autographed! — and the thousands of souvenirs to which it has given rise: miniature Eiffel Towers, the tower on pens, on plates, sculpted towers — all going off every year to be locked away in someone's drawerful of souvenirs in countries all over the world. If we need further proof of her fame, there is always the folk-lore

◀ *The 17th century Institut de France which houses the French Academy. New members are received "under the dome".*

A quiet little square, where a couple of benches and an old street lamp create the old-world charm of the place Furstenberg, just behind Saint-Germain-des-Prés.

that follows in fame's wake. Paris is always full of stories about her; from that of the madman who, at the turn of the century tried to fly from the top platform (he even allowed his ridiculous tragic attempt to be filmed), to the regular April fool stories of the danger of imminent collapse, or the speed with which the tower is sliding into the Seine. There is a whole aura of legend about the tower, but if you see it standing shrouded in rain or fog, gradually disappearing from view or, on a clear night, its warning beacon shining out across the city, you will not find it hard to understand why.

Like the new Pompidou Centre at Beaubourg, which has recently taken its place at the top of the popularity poll of Paris monuments, the Eiffel Tower was,

The "old Lady" of Paris will be a hundred years old in 1989 and her silhouette still dominates the Paris skyline.

What a shock this metal monster must have been to the people who lived on the banks of the Seine!

The superb classical facade of the ▶ *hôtel des Invalides guarded by its row of ancient cannons.*

at the time it was built, just as violently opposed. The artists of the time wrote petition after petition demanding the removal of this "monster" which was disfiguring the landscape. Fortunately the monster survived and soon it will be celebrating its hundredth birthday, since it was built in 1889 for the World Exhibition, overshadowing the classical beauty of the 18th century École Militaire and the architectural innovations of the Unesco building.

But our final visit as we leave the *7e arrondissement* — and the faubourg — must be to the Invalides, that superb monument which is now high up on the ten buildings in France worth preserving at any cost. Everything here, without exception, is outstanding: from the row of cannons in front of the main façade which reminds us that after all this is a military establishment, and the various museums with their military trophies, to the magnificent church of Saint-Louis, the Soldiers' church, where every year a ceremony is held on the anniversary of Napoleon's death. His tomb is in the crypt under the dome, and the return of his ashes in 1840 was the occasion of a national triumph. But it is the simple facade of the hôtel des Invalides which is so exceptionally beautiful. The hospital was built between 1671 and 1676 by Libéral Bruant and thereafter left to the mercy of the elements, so that over the centuries it acquired a thick coating of grime which stained the natural gold of the stone to a murky grey. Then came the great campaign to clean up Paris and we have had to get used to seeing it restored to its original colour. At first it seemed almost too new, but gradually a light patina of dust settled on it again so that today the two hundred metres of this splendid façade are an unbelievably wonderful sight, their only ornament, apart from the great curved arch of the central gateway, being the stone pilasters and suits of armour which frame the long row of the mansard lights above the classical line of the main windows. ∎

71

The shadow of the "little corporal" watches over the main courtyard. Napoleon's tomb in the open crypt under the dome.

Not far from the Invalides, on the other side of the boulevard, the hôtel Biron, Rodin's last home which contains most of his works.

Prolonging the view from the Invalides, whose dome is visible in the distance, is Paris's most elegant bridge, the pont Alexandre III with its decorative lamps and rich ornamentation. ▶

FROM THE PLACE DE LA CONCORDE TO THE ETOILE, this is Paris at her most triumphant, proclaiming her full glory. "The most beautiful avenue in the world", nearly two thousand metres of dazzling brilliance that adds so much to the wonderful view from the Louvre. It is the high spot of any visit to Paris with all its "three-stars" attractions, from the hôtel Crillon to Fouquet's, from the Obelisk to the Arc de Triomphe. The whole nation has taken this great avenue to her heart, and for almost two hundred years now, France has lived and relived the most important moments of her history here. The place de la Concorde was the site of the guillotine during the Reign of Terror, and as we stand on the balconies that surround the square, we can almost imagine we are witnessing the executions of Louis XVI and his queen, Marie-Antoinette. Fortunately today the only scaffolds erected there are for the processions on the 14th of July, the great national holiday, when the whole avenue is given over to official parades, culminating in the traditional march-past and review of the troops. Obviously, there is only one place where such a march could begin — from the Arc de Triomphe, with a dramatic fly-over of air-force jets leaving their tricolore vapour-trails! From the Arc de Triomphe, where the flame over the unknown soldier's tomb burns eternally, and solemn detachments of war veterans in full military dress meet to remember the dead! The public crowd every inch of the route hoping to catch a glimpse of the Alpine Corps with their dogs, the slow march past of the Légionnaires, the young officers from Saint-Cyr and Polytechnique wearing their pointed caps or the more recently created women's units, as the procession moves down to the bottom of the Champs-Elysées where the President of the Republic takes the salute.

De Gaulle came down the Champs-Elysées amidst the rejoicing of the whole nation on the 26th of August, 1944 to celebrate the Liberation of Paris with General Leclerc and all his other comrades-in-arms. Since then, newly inaugurated presidents and visiting heads of state have customarily received the same treatment — it was even accorded to the Saint-Etienne football team after their honourable defeat in Glasgow! But in 1968, when the crowds were demonstra-

back on the Champs-Elysées...

The most famous of the groups of statuary which decorate the Arc de Triomphe, the "Marseillaise" by the sculptor Rude. Other groups between them portray the whole history of France from the Revolution to the Liberation with the national flag flying in their midst.

ting their support for the general, it was from Concorde to the Etoile that the procession went, and so it was to be again two years later when the same crowds expressed their grief at his death.

But it is not merely the political processions and state occasions which give the Champs-Elysées its unchallenged prestige in the eyes of the world. Whenever you walk up the avenue towards the Arc de Triomphe — which is the way most people go — it is the architectural perfection of its converging lines which first attracts the attention and fully justifies its claim to glory. For in the great wide-open spaces of the avenue there are few buildings: just Gabriel's two splendid colonnaded pavilions on the north side of the place de la Concorde with a view of the Madeleine's elegant neo-classical

The Elysée Palace seen from the gardens through the "Coq" gate. Previously the residence of 18th century financiers it has been the official residence of the French President since 1873.

◄ *A dramatic view of the place de la Concorde looking past the Obelisk to the Ministry buildings designed by Gabriel and the Madeleine in the distance.*

The statue of Clemenceau opposite the Grand Palais which was built for the great exhibition of 1900. It is halfway between Concorde and the Rond-Point on the Champs-Elysées.

The Arc de Triomphe in all its ▶
glory.

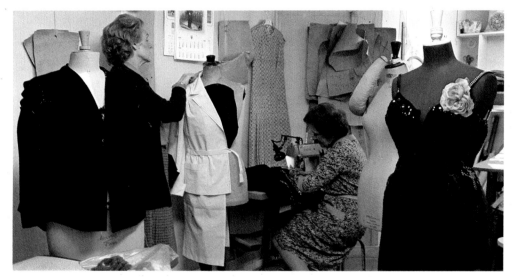

facade at the top of the rue Royale
between them. Then just at the other
end of what appears to be a tree-lined
park full of greenery — it is only an
optical illusion which makes it look so
near — rises the vast, grandiose arch
over which the tricolore flag of France
so often flies. The beautifully sculpted
Marly horses frame the view at the Concorde end of the avenue, and as you pass
between them you almost feel as though
you are setting off for a walk in the
country. There are little pagodas tucked
away among the trees — just made for
lovers' rendez-vous and all the stalls
and amusements of a country fair await
you. Do you want an ice-cream? Or a
donkey ride? Would you like to see the
Punch and Judy show? All is just as it
was in Proust's childhood days. And
for the grown-ups, from the time of the
Second Empire right up to the outbreak
of the First World War, taking a stroll up
the tree-lined Champs-Elysées was the
fashionable thing to do. At the Rond-
Point, everything changes. We are
among the bright lights of today:
surrounded by expensive cinemas showing the latest films, grand cafés and restaurants with their cabarets, luxuriously
tempting shop-windows — all designed
to attract the cosmopolitan jet set who fre-
quents this stretch of the avenue. There
are also the banks, the airlines offices
and tourist companies who have moved
up here to acquire a prestige address for
themselves, not realizing that by doing
so they have completely destroyed the
atmosphere of the old Champs-Ely-

*Haute-Couture in the boutiques
and workrooms of the faubourg
Saint-Honoré.*

*The name of Dior stands out in
this elegant world.*

sées. Ten years ago it was a joy to stroll up here at any time of the day or night — on the right-hand pavement, of course, for that was the fashionable side! But nowadays, when the shops and offices close, there is nothing left at night except the gradually emptying pavements and lights going out one after another in the office blocks. It is all rather sad...

But nonetheless it is still an elegant district with its wide streets and expensive shops, all very pleasant to look at, but on too vast a scale for a comfortable stroll on foot. This world, built during the Second Empire, was not made for pedestrians, and it is only when you are in a car — or standing on top of the Arc de Triomphe! — that you can appreciate the superb planning of the twelve broad avenues which radiate from the Etoile, some of them leading back into the tightly knit heart of the city, others out to leafy suburbs and new horizons. But the swirling traffic round the arch itself is a motorist's nightmare, especially at peak hours!

Not far away is the parc Monceau with its statues and colonnades, its island-studded lake and its magnificent aromatic trees, watched over by the Cernuschi museum with its wonderful collection of oriental treasures.

A little further on still, looking down over the fantastic pattern of railway lines splaying out from the gare Saint-Lazare, is the "European quarter" whose street names send the imaginative passer-by off to dream of Madrid, Naples, Edinburgh, Stockholm...

But the further away from the Champs-Elysées we move, the duller the *8e arrondissement* becomes — typically "right-bank" and not at all interesting. Great boulevards like Haussmann and Saint-Honoré are surrounded by blocks of undistinguished buildings in more modest streets, all of them very "chic" but decidedly monotonous. There is little of the atmosphere and spirit of Paris here!

So the best thing we can do is to head back down towards the Seine on the other side of the Champs-Elysées and recapture that real Paris air, which it is so good to breathe again, on the café terraces between the avenue Georges V and the avenue Montaigne. ∎

The Wallace fountains, the gift of ▶ an American millionaire, were originally intended to provide fresh drinking water for thirsty passers-by. Today it is a nostalgic reminder of a by-gone era.

The neo-classical facade of the Madeleine at the top of the fashionable rue Royale.

AS THE RINGS WHICH MARK the successive stages of its growth become steadily wider, Paris continues to turn about itself — and we shall follow the next coil of our spiral. From now on our boundaries will be on one hand, the circle of the great boulevards built on the site of the city's first ramparts and on the other hand, parallel boulevards just as wide and airy but a little further out, nearer the city's perimeter.

Our journey round her spiral of *arrondissements* will continue with the *9ᵉ* which lies half in the plain and half on the slope leading up to the hills on Paris's northern boundary. It is a kind of border country between the elegance we have just seen in the *8ᵉ* and the densely populated *10ᵉ* and *11ᵉ arrondissements* which still lie ahead of us. It might even be compared with the legendary "City" of her rival capital across the Channel. But this is a typically French "City", where unexpected ingredients are mixed in a bizarre cocktail only made palatable by the incredible vivacity we find here. In the angle of the boulevard Haussmann and the rue Lafayette, which both change completely in character further along, this part of the *9ᵉ* is essentially a business quarter. Most of the banks and insurance companies are here, together with the big dealers in precious stones and antiques. The chief trade unions, serious quality newspapers like *le Monde,* and the auction rooms *(l'hôtel des Ventes)* are based here too. These are all major enterprises housed in distinctly uninteresting premises. There is nothing to alleviate the serious "City" atmosphere which is evident everywhere, nothing to brighten the plainly functional facades of the buildings, nothing to enliven the hushed quiet of the side streets, nothing to distinguish the almost identically nondescript men who, whether they be employers or employees, run this vast financial machine. It is true that the ornately decorated headquarters of the Société-Générale, and the dazzling Maison Dorée now occupied by the Banque Nationale de Paris stand out from the rest, but they are the rare exceptions here, where all other activities seem to take place unobtrusively behind thick walls and locked doors. The jewellers are hidden away on upper floors at a safe height, where no one can see them delicately extracting sapphires and

the Opéra

The elaborately decorated roof of the Opera House, actually as high as Notre-Dame, and here from this angle looking on equal terms with the Sacré-Cœur.

rubies from their protective silk bags — in much the same way as the bank notes and share certificates are silently handled in the B.N.P. next door.

In the other half of the *arrondissement* though, a completely different world takes over — a world where everything

The camera, by shortening the actual perspective of the avenue, has enhanced the visual impact of the Opera House facade with its columns and loggia and the statues of Apollo brandishing his lyre above the massive dome.

"La Danse" by Carpeaux, the famous group of statuary which shocked official prudery when it first appeared on the façade of the Opera house.

is noise, bright lights, crowded streets and unceasing activity: Christmas decorations lighting up the streets of the boulevard Haussmann, the sales in January, the summer "Collections", all mean fresh window displays to attract customers. This is the city's main shopping centre where dozens and dozens of boutiques and shops of all kinds flourish — all selling more or less the same things — around the permanent centrepiece of the famous Printemps and Galeries Lafayette, those huge department stores which sell everything under the sun and even spill out on the pavements too, to the annoyance of motorists and passersby alike.

Thus we have the two contrasting faces of this area, finance and trade. And for good measure, there are the prostitutes too who camp here day and night amid this frenzied activity, all along the shopping streets, leaning against the shop windows, draping themselves across your car bonnet, calmly waiting for custom. Even the Chaussée-d'Antin, once one of the smartest streets in Paris, has now been taken over by shops selling ready-made clothes. This street runs up to the monumental église de la Trinité, but there are also other smaller and far more attractive churches, like Notre-Dame-de-Lorette for example. Further along we come to the Casino de Paris and the place Clichy and then to all the sleazy night-clubs of the bottom end of the place Pigalle. The Nouvelle-Athènes, which was the centre of an artistic and intellectual revival at the end of the 19th century when it was still full of charm and an old-world elegance, has now been invaded by strip-tease joints and gone right downhill. Even though high finance is the main concern of the 9e that does not mean that there is no amusement or relaxation to be had there! There are the oriental patisseries, bistros selling frites, a few shady night-clubs and even a few decent theatres. Then side by side we come across the two high spots of Paris night life, famous the world over, such is their reputation! — the Folies Bergère whose near-naked dancers in their rustling frou-frou skirts need no introduction, and the Palace, that Mecca of the swinging youth of Paris who come in to the big city from far and wide to drink and dance the night away.

But let us forget all this frenzied search for pleasure and move on to the only genuine monument in this part of the city: the Opera House, a splendid building of breath-taking magnificence. It was created by Garnier during the Second Empire and the familiar lines of its richly decorated façade dominate the end of the concourse leading up to it. With its columns and arcades, its loggia which is flood-lit on gala occasions, Carpeaux's "La Danse" sculpture, and the busts of famous musicians — all under the great bronze dome — the façade alone is almost as spectacular as the show we are going in to see. The interior of the theatre is no less beautiful with its vast white marble staircase, its immense colonnaded foyer and the auditorium itself, all red and gold. It is worth arriving early just to be able to sit and admire the Chagall ceiling and the incredible chandelier suspended below it, before the lights are dimmed and interest turns to the performance down there on the stage.

Outside though, life goes on. Exhaust fumes from the serried lanes of slow-moving cars fill the air, never-ending crowds clog the great boulevards which lead down from the Madeleine past the Opera House towards the place de la République and the place de la Nation. And every couple of hours or so the police come round to move them all on... ∎

The great marble staircase leading up to the auditorium on a grand gala occasion... guards with drawn swords line the onyx balustrades.

The Chagall ceiling which has dominated the auditorium since 1964. (FOLLOWING PAGE.)

J'aime flâner sur les grands boulevards
Il y a tant de choses, tant de choses à voir!

"LOVE TO STROLL ALONG the grands boulevards, there are so very many things to see". So sang Yves Montand in the fifties, a song which brings back memories of that other older pre-war refrain: *Le samedi soir, après le turbin, l'ouvrier parisien...* (Saturday night after work the Paris workman...)

Ever since the 18th century, strolling along the tree-lined boulevards of Paris has been the fashionable thing to do. With the 19th century, new cafés sprang up all along them, elegant ones to begin with, then as tastes changed, so the elegant cafés changed too, to become the *cafés-théâtres* and *cafés-concerts* so popular on Saturday nights. Today the boulevards are still as popular as ever, and the discerning observer can trace clear lines of social demarcation as he strolls from one end to the other of them. From the Madeleine to the Opéra the boulevards still have a luxurious 19th century elegance with their fashionable boutiques and the grand buildings of the great business houses; and also, hard by the Opéra, rather like a dazzling shop-window of the Grand Hotel, the recently renovated Café de Paris still delightfully preserves the atmosphere of days gone by.

Beyond the Opéra on the boulevard des Italiens, there may be a few cinemas and drug-stores, but the same feeling of wealth and good taste is still there, though the lovely old-fashioned cafés have all gone. The only survivor from that bygone era is the Opéra Comique, a huge building set a little back from the boulevard. Elsewhere car parks and office blocks have taken over.

The Richelieu-Drouot crossroad is a turning point for the boulevards, both literally and even more markedly "atmospherically". Montmartre, Poissonnière, Bonne-Nouvelle, Saint-Denis and Saint-Martin, leading down to République, are the real boulevards Yves Montand sang about. They belong in a very special way to the people of Paris who flock here in their milling thousands. A few theatres, several cinemas showing "blue" films and endless café-bars flood the pavements with their neon lights. But it is on the boulevards themselves that the surging crowds find their real happiness, rather than in the brightly-lit cafés and bars, though these do indeed create a warmer, more lively atmosphere. Satur-

on the grands boulevards

The other attraction in the 9ᵉ arrondissement — the Folies-Bergère, the titles of whose shows always contain thirteen letters like its own name.

day night is naturally the high spot of the week, when cars and pedestrians jostle for right of way as crowds of people — not a few of them rather drunk — pour in and out of cinemas and cabarets, bars and dance-halls in their feverish search for excitement and pleasure.

Inevitably of course, the prostitutes are here too, around the porte Saint-Denis and the porte Saint-Martin, whose triumphal arches were erected in honour of Louis XIV. All along the famous Strasbourg-Saint-Denis area and on the streets leading down from the gare du Nord and the gare Saint-Lazare towards the Halles, they ply their trade. This is the "red light" district made famous by Henry Miller in his notorious "Tropic of Cancer". And it is a truly amazing sight — it may be a universal one, but it never fails to astound — to see, both in the narrow back streets and on the main boulevards, so many strange-looking creatures in their seductive costumes — the traditional vamp with her plunging neckline, the would-be Amazon in her synthetic leopard skin! Then the

The porte Saint-Denis, built honour of Louis XIV.

One of the Morris columns which advertise shows and concerts in Paris.

The grand boulevards in close-up with their neon signs above crowded pavements.

94 scene suddenly changes completely like a "fade-out" in a film. We leave all this behind when we reach the boulevard Saint-Martin, for between here and the place de la République we are in a busy working-class district.

These people and their little shops and workrooms were with us all the time but they were relegated to the back streets of Saint-Denis among the narrow alleyways and the street markets. Here they are up on the raised pavements (a relic of the old ramparts) in full view, calmly working in spite of the non-stop activity around them, quietly making up their suits and dresses in the work-rooms of their little tailoring shops.

The place de la République, the focal point of this part of the city, is a regular rallying point for the big worker demonstrations, on May Day of course, and also every time the unions want to make social or political demands. And from République, the route these marches always follow takes them down to the place de la Bastille and into the typically working-class quarters round it.

If the "Bastoche" has today been taken over by a battalion of motorcyclists, it is still the home of the Paris *titis* or *gavroches* — the Parisian equivalent of the London Cockney — and the days of the "Balajo" where lithe Apache types danced the java to the sound of wailing accor-

dions are not so very far away. This, along with the streets round the boulevards Richard-Lenoir and Voltaire in the *9e arrondissement,* is the real Paris of the people, with their unmistakable accent, their slang and their working-class traditions.

The winged statue of Liberty looks down on them all from the top of her column, which is a memorial to the 1830 revolution. But of that other Revolution, which flared up one 14th of July, when an inflamed mob tore down the gates of a prison in a symbolic gesture to free a handful of forgotten prisoners, there is not the slightest trace. Only the name remains... nothing more!

◀ *A lock on the Saint-Martin canal right in the heart of Paris — a haven of tranquillity just a stone's throw away from the city's traffic.*

A quiet stroll in the Bois de Vincennes.

The focal point of the place de la République.

A mass demonstration in the place de la Bastille.

Now our path takes us along yet more boulevards, first into the Saint-Antoine district, famous for centuries for its carpenters and cabinet-makers, then on to the last of the great *places* on our route, the place de la Nation. At its centre stands the "Triomphe de la République" yet another statue whose mythological, therefore pagan subject underlines the determinedly anti-clerical philosophy of the post-revolutionary authorities who commissioned it. We have already noticed the same trend in other statues we have seen.

But since the *12ᵉ* is the first in our spiral of *arrondissements* to reach the suburbs, let us turn our backs on Paris for a moment and look at the view framed by those two tall columns which now mark the beginning of the Cours de Vincennes. Away in the distance we can see the Bois de Vincennes itself, an extensive wooded region to the east of Paris, with its castle, its lakes, its zoo and its floral gardens. The famous *Foire du Trône*, originally known as the "Gingerbread Fair" was transferred out to the Bois in 1965 after it had been held for over a thousand years in the former *barrière* of Le Trône, hard by the place de la Nation.

Since the departure of its fair, the *12ᵉ* has not much left to offer the visitor, except the somewhat neglected charm of its trees, a few quite pleasant squares and its almost provincial calm. Eventually it will lead us back to the Seine where we shall find a different world, the world of the old "villages" of Paris which we shall explore on our next expedition.

95

All the fun of the fair! "The Foire ▶ du Trône", the most ancient and the most famous fair in Paris, now banished from the Trône (place de la Nation) to the Bois de Vincennes.

AS WE MOVE INTO THE NEXT nine *arrondissements,* this inventory of Paris is nearing its end. From here onwards, the spiral we have been following right from the start of our journey reaches its outer limits which are defined by the *boulevards des Maréchaux* round the perimeter of the city — Ney, Berthier, Lannes, Suchet, Murat and so on. They are all named after Napoleon's victorious field-marshalls. These boulevards formed the final ring round Paris until the creation of the *boulevard périphérique* just beyond them encircled the city completely with a fast expressway. A special bus route, the P.C. (the only route to have kept its letters instead of changing over to numbers), runs round the whole thirty-five kilometres of this final perimeter. It connects on its way all the old city gates thus recalling the days of the *octrois,* check points where all goods into and out of the city were rigorously controlled as if at an international frontier.

Today, access to the city is unrestricted — in fact it is not always easy to tell exactly where the densely populated city *arrondissements* finish and the adjacent suburbs begin, for they are all equally built up with supermarkets and H.L.M. But in 1860, when Napoleon III's government decided quite simply to annex the villages of this final coil of our spiral, things were very different. A series of fifty-seven *barrières* had been created by the architect Ledoux on the line of the old boundary of the *fermiers-généraux.* The term *barrière* to mean a district is no longer used except here and there in the provinces (for example, in Bordeaux), but Ledoux's "barrières" clearly marked the city limits with a series of neo-classical villas. Beyond this limit, in what are now the heavily built-up *arrondissements* we shall be visiting on the rest of our journey there was the occasional village, but most of the land was either under the plough or wooded, with the odd farm, patches of waste ground and a quarry or two. The whole of this green belt quite naturally attracted the fresh-air-starved Parisians who came out on week-end excursions or even built country cottages here — long before the term "résidences secondaires" had been invented.

But gradually the villages were devoured by the city. It is hard today to imagine people going out to the "fields"

the ancient villages of Paris

In the villages south of Paris you can still find the old wooden shack hidden in the surrounding undergrowth — an anachronism in this 20th century.

of Auteuil. A few places have kept their evocative names — le Petit-Montrouge is one — and Saint-Mandé has not changed all that much since it became part of the city. But apart from one or two exceptions like these, one has to dig deep into local history to appreciate the fact that each of these districts was once a real village with a rural atmosphere all its own. A few of these fresh "oases" can still be found, but we must tread gently through them or their fragile old-world charm will be shattered. For example, although it is now dominated by a highrise block of luxury flats, the market in the place d'Aligre is still a real country market with its wholesome-looking food stalls, its flowers and its piles of bric-à-brac on the pavements. You can still, if you ignore the obtrusive buildings round about you, wander around the narrow streets and the bistros and feel you are in a lively little provincial town.

Shall we go for a ride on the *Train Bleu* a few hundred yards down the road? No need to hurry to catch this train — no need to bother about the Mistral or the T.G.V. — for this journey will only take us back in time. For this *Train Bleu*, with its embroidered curtains, lofty moulded ceilings and the delightful naïveté of the Mediterranean scenes painted on its walls by painters fashionable at the time, takes us back to 1901 when the restaurant was first opened. It still has the same old tables and benches, and the frock-coated maître d'hôtel, the waiters in their white jackets and the lady at the cash-desk in her severe black suit look as though they have been here ever since the place opened.

Now we must cross the Seine to continue this nostalgic journey — for everything has changed so much — through the one-time villages on the south of the river which are now the 13^e, 14^e and 15^e *arrondissements* contained within a great loop of the river. They all seem strangely alike. It is almost as if we were going through a series of identical little towns: a wide and busy main road through, which every now and then sprouts a sheaf of little side-streets to form a small provincial town within a town. Each has its square which often boasts a now disused bandstand and is filled with market stalls two or three times a week. And each of these mini-towns has its "mediaeval" church — built in the last century — and its "mairie", 1880 model, echoing on a smaller scale the imitation Renaissance ostentation of the Hôtel de Ville in central Paris.

Successive waves of demolition work, clearing the way for more and more traffic and more and more building, have practically submerged these former villages. Very often nothing remains of them but their names: Poterne-des-Peupliers, Butte-aux-Cailles, Port-Royal, Plaisance... to remind us of these little communities swallowed up in the maw of the city. Among all this jumble of illassorted buildings, the traditional atmosphere of these different little pockets of life has struggled to survive, as if everyone realised how important it was to safeguard these little enclaves, where you still stop and chat to your neighbours in the street and feel part of a community.

The squares and markets play a great part in this, and there is considerable rivalry between one small district and the next. Anyone who shops in the rue Lecourbe will look down his nose at the rue du Commerce. Five hundred yards along the road, and you might be in a different world. And this neighbourhood spirit is some small compensation for the anonymity of the office blocks in the city centre where most of these people have to go to work.

Not very much of real merit stands out from this higgledy-piggledy sea of houses and shops, though there are just one or two things it would be a pity to miss. For example, it was Libéral Bruant, the architect of the Invalides, who built the chapel of the hospital of the Salpêtrière, and Perrault, one of the architects of the Louvre, who built the Observatory. Some of the original Gobelins workshops and parts of the abbey of Port-Royal still stand to this day. These are all in the 13e and 14e *arrondissements.* In the 15e, the largest of these three on the south of the river, there is virtually nothing of real interest except some rather pleasant villas and the studios of the artists of the contemporary Paris school. We must linger here on the borders between the 14e and 15e *arrondissements* for immediately we say Paris School we think of Montparnasse, the only cross-roads in this part of Paris which can hold a candle to Saint-Germain or Montmartre. If we follow the axis into the city from the porte d'Orléans we are not far from the Cité Universitaire with its motley collection of pavilions and its international student population. Opposite it is the parc Montsouris in the neighbourhood of which some artists, including Braque, have lived. Created in the last century, the park's main interest lies in the variety of botanical species grown in its gardens, and in its calm green lawns which re-echo the long belt of parks, sports grounds and cemeteries on the far edge of the boulevards. The trees in the avenue René-Coty seem to make it almost an extension of the park as we head up towards Denfert-Rochereau, presided over by Bartholdi's lion. This is an attractive square with its elegant Ledoux houses on one hand and the noisy animation reigning in the nearby street market on the other.

Now we are in the boulevard Raspail which takes us up from the school of architecture, past the American Centre and Rodin's statue of Balzac, right into the heart of Montparnasse, to the rue Vavin. It was here that the pre-1914 "revolutionaries" and the artists and intellectuals of those frenzied years before and after the First World War lived:

Montparnasse — la Coupole, a fashionable rendez-vous.

Lenin, Cendrars, Miller, Hemingway, Modigliani, Foujita, Kandinsky and the many others who frequented the Coupole, the Rotonde and the Dôme and turned the artistic world upside down. What hair-raising stories could be told of their wild parties, their fiercely held opinions on life and art, and the debauchery which ruined many of their lives! The war took away artists and their models alike, but today Montparnasse after twenty years in the wilderness, has recovered some of that noisy pre-war animation and atmosphere, for the area round that incongruous 200 metres tower has been largely redesigned. But right on the edge of the *arrondissement* there is still Bobino's, the Closerie des Lilas, and the little cemetery where Baudelaire is buried.

Once again, all roads lead to the Seine which we shall have to cross once more — and for the last time — if we are to visit the rest of these villages round the edge of Paris. There, on the left bank of the river, to the west of the capital, as if they were trying to compete with the gigantic monstrosities perpetrated round the place d'Italie to the east, huge blocks of enormous skyscrapers have eroded more and more of the skyline since the 1970s and they are still multiplying in number. It is like a pre-view of Paris in the 21st century... The waterfront of the Seine is a megalomaniac array of identical facades, though here admittedly there is some slight variety of colour and texture in the materials used. In this "pilot" area where the monstrous Centre Beaugrenelle displays the full horror of its interminable stairways, its innumerable shops and arcades, we really do need to escape back in time to those simple villages. So let us cross the river quickly... ■

The incongruous Montparnasse tower... two hundred metres of smoked glass redeemed only by the dazzling effect it presents at night.

A rural corner of old Montparnasse.

The French sculptor Bartholdi ▶ *designed the Statue of Liberty in New York harbour and this replica, standing on the waterfront of the Seine at Grenelle was presented to Paris as a token of gratitude for the original work.*

UNTIL COMPARATIVELY RECENTLY the *16ᵉ arrondissement,* which comprises the former villages of Auteuil and Passy, was far and away the most sought-after residential district in Paris and property there commanded the highest prices in the capital. But a shortage of housing there, the enormous rise in property values and the limited area available for building in the *arrondissement* itself, were just a few of the factors which led to an increase in rents in other parts of Paris. The Champ-de-Mars (Paris *7ᵉ*), Luxembourg (Paris *6ᵉ*) and a few more select districts joined Passy and Auteuil at the top of the price league and challenged its exclusivity.

But Auteuil and Passy have kept a certain aura of elegant refinement which still attracts a very socially conscious type of resident regardless of price. The *16ᵉ* is the home of the wealthy bourgeoisie, snobbish and often pretentious; but at the same time it has an air of decidedly aristocratic distinction. Even the P. et T. (the Post Office) have recognized its pre-eminence, for it is the only one of Paris's twenty *arrondissements* to have two post codes: 75016 and 75116.

The site itself is one of the most beautiful in the city, built on two hills between the Seine and the Bois de Boulogne, with a nice easy slope up into Auteuil and a rather steeper one into Passy, or to the Etoile through Chaillot, a third one-time village, better known to fans of the theatre as the home of the legendary T.N.P. (Théâtre National Populaire) and its stars Jean Vilar and Gérard Philipe. Here, in Chaillot, there is elegance in profusion on the luxurious avenue Victor-Hugo with its expensive houses and shops, and on the fashionable avenue Foch where it is considered the height of elegance to walk always on the sunny side of the street! Even the prostitutes here and around the Etoile are among the most superior to be found in Paris!

As we head back from Chaillot towards Passy, we shall find the same world of private houses and blocks of flats stretched out along pleasant tree-lined avenues. Everything here is "chic", everything is in the best of taste, and ostentation is limited to the exclusive receptions, dinners and cocktail parties at which this elegant world entertains itself. So it is amusing to see the fortunate owners of these luxury abodes deign-

from Grenelle to Passy

*A rather dated neo-classical figure
from the Museum of Modern Art.*

Balzac's house in Auteuil, now a museum.

On the lake in the Bois de Boulogne.

ing go along in person to fill jugs and bottles with the genuine spa water which bubbles to the surface in the square Lamartine. And their wives and charming daughters can often be seen too, jug in hand, in the rue de Passy or crossing the Ranelagh gardens bordering on the *Bois* — as the Bois de Boulogne is affectionately known.

In the 18th century, following the king's example, this quarter was the scene of many a secret encounter. Today however, wandering quietly among the shops, watching the ladies in Franck et Fils — a sort of up-market Galeries Lafayette — or drinking tea at Coquelin's, one could imagine oneself back in the golden age of the Proustian bourgeoisie, as if two world wars, socialism and the rise of the working classes had never happened.

Auteuil, on the other hand, which ends at the Muette, at the top of the avenue Mozart, is another matter, for it has all the charm of a simple provincial town. Money is again only too apparent in the luxury dwellings, the peaceful villas and the "hamlets" where one can still lead an almost rural life, in a quiet neighbourhood where the birds make more noise than the car hooters even though one is so near the heart of the city. This is a real village, and business is run on traditional family lines. The baker's is

right next door to the church, which explains why everybody leaves Mass clutching flimsy cardboard packages... Auteuil is an historic place as well. Molière, Boileau and Racine came here to the Mouton Blanc, a delightful little restaurant the like of which you will not find anywhere else within a radius of a hundred miles nowadays. Auteuil once had its own vineyards, and springs of spa water to which people would come from miles around to sample their healing properties on medical advice. What a marvellous excuse it must have been for the 18th century Parisians to leave the crowded capital and relax for a brief while in the country! For before Paris's hideous skyscrapers reared their ugly heads, one could really imagine oneself deep in the country here, as one visited Balzac's house, for example, a little rustic pavilion perched halfway up the hill and commanding marvellous views over the plain beyond the river.

Auteuil is also probably the only place in Paris to have benefited from the architectural achievements of the last hundred years — if we forget about the Maison de la Radio, the Palais-gruyère as it was derisively nicknamed, which was not exactly a success! It has interesting houses designed by Le Corbusier and Mallet-Stevens — the latter in particular on starkly functional cubist lines. And

it also had Guimard, the prince of the Art Nouveau movement. The rue de la Fontaine and all the surrounding streets are like an open-air Art Nouveau museum. They display all the enchanting madness of that whimsical movement as interpreted by its most genial exponent, who cheerfully broke all the rules of geometry in the profusion of arabesques, ornamental windows and delightfully tortured balconies he created. He was also responsible for those glorious metro entrances which were once the joy of Paris, and of which one or two still remain.

Such is the *16e arrondissement,* set against the backdoor of the Bois. And once we have passed the last of the palatial houses, probably the ultimate in luxury for the privileged few, we are in the Bois de Boulogne proper, which seems like an *arrondissement* in its own right, so vast is the expanse of trees interspersed with lakes and green swathes of grass stretching down towards the Seine at its southern edge. But the famous Bois lives two completely separate lives. By day, especially in the fine weather, it is one huge family playground. By night it becomes the scene of a frenzied search for dubious pleasures.

Thus, during the daytime, the Bois is alive with a whole host of people: elegant sporting types from the Racing Club, and jogging keep-fit enthusiasts; mothers pushing their prams; folk who have come there to ride, or to take a boat out on the lake, or just to admire the flowers and the gardens. And on Sundays whole families come to picnic there, to play their innocent games and enjoy its wide-open spaces. At such times motorists pass by on the new expressway without so much as a glance at all this activity, and if they begin to slow down as night falls, it is only because the peak time hold-ups at the exits from Paris do not make any exception for the road through the Bois.

But later in the evening it is a very different kind of traffic which invades the Bois. Cars crawl past at a walking pace as their drivers examine the shadowy figures of the women purposefully lingering by the roadsides, offering occasional enticing glimpses of their all too available charms. Other cars are parked, silently, disturbingly, in the darkness, like so many sinister threats. And if headlights cut through the night, they may well pick out one after another of the "prowlers" in their slow-moving cars, the plain-clothes policemen and their quarry — those shadowy women of the night who haunt the trees.

Tomorrow morning though, the sunlight will stream through the trees again and everything will be bright and cheerful once more. ∎

Punters at the Auteuil race-course.

The spectacular fountains at the porte de Saint-Cloud.

There are still a few romantic spots on the cobble-stoned quays of the Seine between the stationary barges and the trees — but the ▶ skyscrapers are coming nearer and nearer.

THE PLACE DE L'ETOILE — or place Charles de Gaulle as we must remember to call it — is our starting point for this last stage of our journey round Paris. We shall go from west to east along the last lap of our spiral. We saw the *16ᵉ* on our last excursion, so today we shall start in the *17ᵉ*. We shall not be tempted to linger very long here, for there is little to interest us and not a trace of its old villages, Ternes and Batignolles. The only thing which alleviates the monotonous impersonality of the *arrondissement* is the luxurious Palais des Congrès at the porte Maillot, to which the avenue de la Grande Armée — the prolongation beyond the Arc de Triomphe of the famous Champs-Elysées leads us. If we look back towards the centre of Paris, we can find traces of greenery in the area round the boulevard Malesherbes, and a faint echo of the old provincial atmosphere, but otherwise all its 19th century charm has gone, and despite the busy shops in the rue de Lévis, this *arrondissement* is extremely dull.

However, a little further out, past the railway at Saint-Lazare, we come to the second belt of boulevards which separates the city from the nearby suburbs, and here at last we rediscover the zest and vigour which has so far been missing. This is because we are crossing over into the *18ᵉ*, and from now on, all the way along the boulevards through the two remaining *arrondissements,* this sense of vitality and energy will be with us.

But this, with one exception, is the end of the regular tourist trail; there are no classical monuments in this densely populated belt where street markets and rather dingy cafés mark our way. But there is such a prodigious variety of life here! So many different types of people, so many different customs, and not a few extremely pleasant places. Our route is now taking us to the real heights of Paris, the ones we noticed as we came into the city from the south, and as we climb higher and higher we shall never tire of the splendid views of the city stretched out beneath us, or of the real freshness of the air up here after the suffocating fumes of the city traffic.

The boulevard des Batignolles is part of a different world which stretches out towards Clichy and Saint-Ouen — long, heavily populated faubourgs on the further slopes of Montmartre. La Fourche,

the heights of Paris

The grape-harvest is still celebrated in Montmartre in memory of the time when it was a country village, planted all over with vineyards and dotted with wind-mills and little chapels.

the rue Ordener, Marcadet-Poissonnière, Château-Rouge mark the beginnings of a vast built-up area beyond the city's actual limits in the midst of which is the Marché aux Puces (the Flea Market) alive with excitement and colour. But it is in the place Clichy, with its inevitable statue — all squares of any importance in Paris have one — that we shall begin the next stage of our journey, from "gay Paris" to "Ménilmuche", and pass as quickly as possible through it for it is one of the most sordid places in the city.

So to the place Clichy, with its "new release" cinemas, its brightly lit bars and its crowds. This is (or was) the "red light" district around Montmartre, along the boulevards Clichy and Rochechouart, with those twin pillars of vice, the place Blanche and Pigalle. The tone of the district has already been set in the place Clichy where an old run-down cinema has been refurbished to show blue films. "Forget your troubles, come and see our sexy films!" run the bill-boards. This is one of the few places in Paris which is on tap twenty-four hours a day and it reaches an absolute low in vulgarity. The sails of the Moulin Rouge may shine glitteringly above it, but they do not disguise the fact that Pigalle is nothing but an immense brothel.

A bit higher up, the air is purer, cleaner... and even if the only thing left

In the shadow of the Sacré-Cœur, the old streets which wind up the hill are a picturesque reminder of the 19th century.

The "Lapin Agile" was once the haunt of poets and artists, and famous cabaret artists like Yvette Guilbert and Jane Avril were painted by Toulouse-Lautrec.

Other memories of the past a enshrined in the wax-wor museum on the hill.

◀ *From a height of over a hundred metres the dazzling white basilica of the Sacré-Cœur looks down over Paris.*

to remind us that Montmartre was once a real country village is the Moulin de la Galette, at least this Bohemian community re-echoes the real charm the village once had. It has been helped to retain its identity by the flights of steps which cut off many of the streets. Everywhere you find those lovely old 19th century street-lamps, chestnut trees, terraces of quiet houses, and of course the inevitable cupolas of the Sacré-Cœur! Here the tourists are with us again in their coach-loads. The basilica is a 19th century monstrosity, but if we turn our backs on it, the view over Paris is stunning from where we stand at a height of 104 metres above the Seine. The picturesque neighbourhood round it — the rue des Saules, the rue Saint-Vincent, the place du Tertre — is still impressively beautiful, even though it has been invad-

The place du Tertre a stone's throw away from the basilica is always crowded with tourists who wander round the colourful open-air exhi-

ed by souvenir shops and would-be artists out to con the tourists. There are a few of the old *cafés-concerts* left, like the Lapin Agile, frequented in the past by real poets and artists and still providing entertainment in the form of the satirical songs of today's *chansonniers*.

bition under the trees. They occasionnally fall for the invitations of the artists and allow their portraits to be painted.

Now we can walk back down the hill through the series of gardens and impressive flights of steps in front of the basilica, or use Paris's one and only funicular railway which runs down alongside them. In either case we shall come out into the marché Saint-Pierre, the best fabric market in the city, where the stall-holders themselves with their cluttered stalls, and the last remaining street hawkers with their barrows, seem straight out of the rue Lepic!

So here we are back on the boulevards with the crowds again. Between Barbès and Stalingrad, and particularly in the region of the Goutte d'Or, whole streets have been taken over by immigrant workers, mainly Arabs and North Africans, who came over in the sixties. This is where they live their lives, buying and selling what they can, playing their games of chance on the pavements — disorientated, rootless exiles who have little to do but desultorily walk about the streets. The whole zone, between the porte de la Chapelle and the porte de la Villette, like its inhabitants, is sad, with

nothing but dismal views of shunting-yards and the bare walls of empty buildings. This is the wretched unseen face of Paris where there is nothing to brighten the depressing picture of slum housing and exploited workers. Nothing at all redeems it and the canal with its murky docks reminds us of the sinister world of Dickens's London.

The crossroad at Stalingrad brings another change of scene. Invaded by the overhead metro, this crossroad between the old *abattoirs* of la Villette and the dismal northern suburbs opens out into the *19e* and *20e* — the last of our twenty *arrondissements*. Here the avenues are wider and a little more reminiscent of the real old-time Paris. Belleville, Ménilmontant! This is the world which spawned Maurice Chevalier, the typical Parisian *titi*, the Paris "Cockney" — or *Parigot,* to use another slang word which means the same thing. This is their birth-place, even more so than the Bastille area where we met them before. But their favourite haunts are fast disappearing. The place des Fêtes is already

Its bistros, its crowds and the sound of accordions filling the air.

dead and the rue de Belleville soon will be, ruined by the massive development which has destroyed people and traditions along with the buildings bulldozed down to make room for more of those hideous concrete cubes.

For the moment, the lovely park of the Buttes-Chaumont has survived, and this is the last of our "heights". From here, at a height of 101 metres, we can look out over the trees and the beautiful facades of the surrounding buildings on to the distant blue horizons of the Ile-de-France. In parts of the Belleville district, near what was once a real village church, there are still a few craftsmen plying their trades, long rows of little houses with well-kept gardens line the quiet back-streets, and there too is the highest point in Paris, the rue du Télégraphe at 128 metres.

Still on the boulevard, near the busy Ménilmontant crossroads, where crescents of handsome apartment blocks curve round the place, Jews and Arabs live peaceably side by side, each following his own kosher practices and spending long hours on the almost Mediterranean-looking café terraces. And we are nearly at the end of our spiral of *arrondissements* now, for the avenue des Pyrénées takes us down past the Père-Lachaise, right to the Cours de Vincennes, where the *20e* joins up with the *12e arrondissement* in which we started this long pilgrimage round the villages and the heights of Paris. We are in the Bois de Vincennes again, that lovely stretch of parkland on the east of Paris which balances so neatly on the map with the Bois de Boulogne on the west. Between them lies the whole great city. ■

A quiet corner of Montmartre where the old village atmosphere still survives. This is the place Emile-Goudeau where the cubism of Picasso, Braque, Matisse and Juan Gris was born.

2
the three ages of Paris

1861 and Haussmann doing his worst! Most of mediaeval Paris was reduced to rubble, including this tower which was part of Philippe-Auguste's wall and had survived intact for five and a half centuries.

"beneath the pavements, a beach..."

LONG AFTER THE STUDENT REVOLTS of '68 had subsided and peace had been restored at the approach of the holidays, graffiti and political slogans still remained on the walls. Some were quite funny, others had serious political messages. One or two were almost lyrical: "Sous les pavés, une plage..." comes to mind. This one seems particularly poignant for it sums up the whole history of the great city — of any city as far as that goes — by reminding us that under all the concrete of urban development, the good earth is still there.

«Under the cobblestones of Paris, a beach...» Before it ever became the cradle of two thousand years of history, part of whose progress we have followed round its twenty *arrondissements,* Paris was already there in the geographical sense — a parcel of land in the part of the world we call Europe. In the beginning, Paris was not the Seine, not the *5ᵉ* or the *9ᵉ arrondissements,* not Pigalle or Saint-Germain — it was simply a stretch of

river, a calcium plateau in an alluvial plain, surrounded by a semi-circle of hills beyond which lay further plateaux. Paris was just forests and lakes, rocky wildernesses and fertile ground. That was Paris before man first challenged nature. Now nature has almost disappeared from the scene, pushed further and further back as the city has grown. She has been destroyed, forced out of sight and mind under a thick layer of concrete. The materials with which nature herself provided man, he has selfishly used to destroy her in the name of civilization. First of all he took her earth and her rocks to cover her pathways and turn them into roads; then he covered these roads with cobblestones, and now they too have disappeared under a rock-hard layer of concrete. The river is now little more than a channel enclosed on both sides by walls of stone, and its banks have been turned into motorways. Nowadays, amid the buildings and the maze of streets and railways, it takes an enormous effort

of the imagination to rediscover the natural relief beneath it all, its slopes, its flat stretches and the ups and downs of its original geological structure. Even the trees did not altogether escape and those which did are often caged in iron railings, or planted in such orderly patterns in parks and gardens that it is hard to believe that they are real.

The whole city has been built on top of nature, rather than alongside her, and there is very little harmony or balance between the two. Pavements, drainage systems and a carpet of streets link the buildings which were once the gypsum and other basic elements in the surrounding soil. Man-made quays, cellars and underground roads have burrowed into the depths of the earth. Noise of every kind meets in an incessant background hum that drowns all natural sounds. Smoke and pollution are forming high up in the atmosphere a layer of dust which is gradually blocking out the sky. Everything and everybody is competing to turn the city into a world beyond the reach of nature. And so it is, not only with Paris, but with all the cities man has made.

But we have not yet quite reached the realms of science-fiction, where people live in plastic, air-conditioned domes lit only by artificial light. Paris still has its changing sky, different each day, its patches of blue suddenly hidden by cloud. Dawn follows dusk as it always has done and there are still days of glorious sunshine as there are days of depressing rain. Sometimes during

An echo of the past as the knife-grinder's cart comes round...

In an attempt to bring some colour and life into the anonymous dehumanized city, the large-scale mural made its appearance on the walls of Paris.

the depressing cycles of weather, nature plays odd tricks on man, leaving him bewildered and helpless. It has only to rain too heavily up-stream for the river to rise and flood his precious motorways and cellars. In 1910 the floods were so bad that the boulevards were like canals, and people could only get around in boats. On the other hand, the temperature has only to drop a few extra degrees for black ice to turn man's roads into skid-pans; for snow to banish his now useless cars back to the shelter of their garages; to turn the man-made lakes in the parks of Paris into marvellous skating-rinks — natural ones at that! Obviously these are exceptional circumstances, but perhaps they can help to remind us that the city can never quite shake off its links with nature for it is still vulnerable to all her changing moods. Sometimes the very place-names bear witness to this fact, names which remind us that where the town is now was once the countryside — names like the Marais, the Butte-aux-Cailles, the rue de la Glacière and so on.

Over such a long period in the history of man, all the different stages of his adaptation to living in cities are superimposed one upon the other. And in these various strata of first geological, and then social development, the traces of Paleolithic or Neolithic life, objects from the bronze age or Gallo-Roman remains like the Arènes de Lutèce or the Roman baths at Cluny are not so very different in their significance from the little patches of green park still to be found here and there in the city, the traces of her previous existences which nature has left behind. Both tell us that before reaching the stage at which we know her today, the city has gone through an evolutionary cycle not unlike that of man who created her.

The few remaining cobblestones, the traces of the old tram-lines, the few acres of vineyard left on the slopes of Montmartre, the last of the craftsmen running the little workshops which no-one will take over from them when they die, the little alleyways and cul-de-sacs, the occasional 14th century house and even the Sunday markets are all memories of lives the great city has lived, of other life-styles, other eras, other people.

But let us not indulge in the facile nostalgia of saying: Ah! In the good old days... If only you had come yesterday! Only 20 years ago! Even if it is true that something very worthwhile has been lost, and lost for ever, let us endeavour to remember that every time something is lost, something equally valuable is born. The city is, and always will be, a living body. ∎

The drains once ran down the middle of narrow dark streets....

from Haussmann to Bienvenüe

THE PASSAGE OF TIME TENDS to blur the various stages in the growth of a great capital like Paris until finally all the changes that have taken place over the centuries become lost in the amorphous mass of the modern city. Our short memories have a tendency to forget the historical past, and only the more recent urban upheavals remain clear in the mind. It is basically true to say that the Paris we know today was built in two stages: the first around 1860 was the work of the Second Empire; the second part of the work was begun in 1960 under the Vth Republic and goes on to this day. But we must never let these two main steps allow us to forget the achievements of every single government in French history, for Paris could not exist in its present form without them. The recent discovery of a section of the first boundary wall built in the 3rd century, should serve to remind us that, long before the investiture of the first Capetian monarch in the 10th century, Paris had already embarked on this long

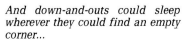

And down-and-outs could sleep wherever they could find an empty corner...

process of reconstruction, development and evolution that has made her the city she is today.

Century after century, each king of France tried to leave his mark on the capital and make it his own. Take the Louvre as an example. Philippe-Auguste began by paving the streets and building the first fortress; Charles V turned the fortress into something more like a palace and installed his famous library; but it was François I who in the 16th century decided that it should be the official residence of the kings of France and transferred his court there from his castles on the Loire and set in motion an extensive building programme. Unfortunately, this was not long before he died, but future rulers, from Henry II to Napoleon III each added his own contribution to the creation of the Louvre we know today. This is just one example, but others come to mind. After Saint-Louis had built the Sainte-Chapelle, Philippe le Bel added the Conciergerie, and his successors, after an official government department responsible for the city had been created, went on to build its boundary walls. New squares, new bridges, new districts appeared every time there was a change of government.

This went on till the 19th century and the aim of each new government was to extend the boundaries of the capital. It was only the Revolutionary Council which destroyed rather than created, and they concentrated on the destruction of monasteries and ecclesiastical property in their bitter struggle with the church. Napoleon himself never had time to put his plans for modernization into practice, so when his nephew came to power in 1851, he found the accumulation of eight centuries of building in which every successive development was detectable.

For we must not forget that on Napoleon III's accession to power, mediaeval Paris, with its tangled web of narrow alleyways and its appalling sanitation, was still very much in evidence alongside the monumental achievements of the great builders. Thus it is perfectly legitimate, historically speaking, to see in the

massive undertakings of Haussmann, a prefect of Paris, the first real revolution in town planning which altered for all time the face of the city. Conceived by the Emperor himself this bold plan was the answer to many real needs.

First of all, France needed a clean, modern, efficient capital to rival those of other European countries. Secondly, Napoleon wanted to eradicate all the tiny alleyways and concentrations of workers that could become a breeding ground for discontent and further revolutions. Whatever the reason behind it though, one fact remains very clear — it was a vast undertaking. It took fifteen years to lay the foundations of the Paris in which we are still living one century later. Paris became one huge building site! The whole town was torn apart, gutted and rebuilt. All the great boulevards were built in one fell swoop: Sébastopol and Saint-Michel, the main north-south axis: Saint-Germain, Opéra, Rivoli; Malesherbes, Haussmann; Magenta; and the vast avenues radiating from the Etoile. We can imagine the scale and speed of the demolition works, all undertaken simultaneously to enable the job of modernization to be done as quickly as possible. Many of the *hôtels* disappeared along with other traces of the Middle Ages, to be replaced by an architecture symbolic of the new era. Imposing bourgeois houses appeared; and new stations, the new Halles, and even the occasional church like Saint-Augustin were built round the same basic structure of metal girders as the Eiffel Tower. Pa-

ris had changed for good. Living standards changed, and sanitation and conditions generally were improved beyond measure, but it was all done at the expense of the environment.

Gas lighting had arrived, asphalt had been invented, the sewers were extended and new bridges were built over the Seine. New roads had to be made to link up the former villages which were annexed in 1860. But the new parks which were planned to brighten this asphalt jungle could in no way make up for the age-old charm of the little streets and gardens which had been demolished, or prevent the mass exodus of the poorer classes from the city to the suburbs when rents in the capital soared sky-high after the programme of renovation.

Paris had become a modern capital, and during the two great exhibitions of 1855 and 1867 the whole world came to admire her, with more than five million visitors in '55 and more than fifteen million twelve years later.

But we can only imagine what the reaction of the public must have been to this massive upheaval. One has only to remember what an uproar of protest there was ten years ago when plans were announced to build a car park under the square in front of Notre-Dame! But apart from the fact that the excavation work revealed undreamed of archaeological treasure, the whole exercise was a mere trifle compared with Haussmann's operations. They resulted in wholesale chaos which must have disrupted thousands of lives. For example, when

119

Tearing down the walls of Paris to make way for Haussmann's rebuilding.

120 Viollet-le-Duc restored Notre-Dame and saved it from falling into ruin the whole area in front of it was completely destroyed. Gone were the little alleyways leading from one street to the next, gone many of the old churches, the huddle of cramped little houses, the teeming life that had been there since the Middle Ages. Everything was flattened, razed to the ground, and all to create an open square in front of the cathedral for which there was no historical precedent.

As for the Opera House and the avenue leading up to it, which today forms one of the most impressive sights in central Paris, one must go back to old photographs taken while the work was in progress to realize to the full just what the project involved. Entire streets of houses were demolished to make room for a broad avenue which would make a fitting approach to the grand new building, and complete the fine prospect from the Palais Royal. What did it matter if half an arrondissement was reduced to rubble in the process? Our photograph shows the facade of the new Opera House dominating a scene of utter destruction all round it — the whole area looks like the aftermath of an earthquake!

After upheavals like this, and bearing in mind the weak position of the 3rd Republic after the defeat of 1870, there was a political motive to encourage the completion of Haussmann's plans, and prestige buildings like the Sacré-Cœur, the tour Eiffel and the rebuilding of the Hôtel de Ville after it was burnt down in 1871, became an urgent priority. Thereafter, in the period leading up to and beyond the 1914 war, the accent was placed on services to improve life in the capital: the water supply, gas and electricity supplies, the sewerage system and a scheme for the removal of household waste. Dustbins were introduced for the first time, called *poubelles* after the name of the Prefect whose brain-child they were.

At last came the crowning achievement — the metro. The 3rd Republic had begun its reign by repairing the ravages of the Commune and its firebombs, yet by the turn of the century it had put into service one of the urban wonders of the world, an underground train network linking the city centre and the suburbs. Fulgence Bienvenüe, inspector general of the Ponts et Chaussées, was the moving spirit behind it and one of the metro stations is named after him. But, however useful and efficient the new service might prove to be, it was a long time before the people of Paris forgot the new round of upheavals it caused. Here again, old photographs speak volumes. The whole city was disembowelled as tracks were laid beneath the city streets. Not even the Seine escaped, for tunnels under the river were an essential part of the system. So, once again, gaping holes and tunnels were dug and millions of cubic metres of earth extracted from the substratum of Paris. Sometimes when underground work proved impossible, the planners tried to design overhead lines which would have crossed some of the city's major junctions and destroyed the privacy of the houses and flats they looked down upon. If all their plans had been accepted — a few of them were — they might even have threatened the façade of the Opera House, but fortunately that plan was scrapped. ∎

Work in progress on the construction of the avenue de l'Opéra.

Today we can forgive Haussmann for the devastation he caused as we view, from the top of the Arc de Triomphe, the remarkable lay-out of the twelve great avenues which radiate from the Etoile.

towards the year 2000

FOR TWENTY YEARS NOW, PARIS has been in the throes of another revolution. But today's revolutionary projects bear strange technical names like P.A.D.O.G. — *Plan d'aménagement et d'organisation générale de la région parisienne*, or S.D.A.U., alias *Schéma directeur d'aménagement et d'urbanisme*. Project after project has been put forward: "scenario for the future", "areas of special study" and so on. The engineers and planners of the 19th century had not exactly been afraid to tear the city to pieces. But their vandalism was as nothing compared with what is going on today, and we look back on their work affectionately, finding its Belle Epoque flavour almost as precious as those Roman paving stones left over from a much earlier age. But today, behind the apparently organised architectural programme, there is indescribable chaos — demolition here, rebuilding there, apparently at random. What is worse, nowadays the problem concerns not only Paris, but the whole Parisian region, which comprises eight departments and over ten million people. Within this "Greater Paris", the original Paris, capital of France, is in danger of losing its identity. Already the distinction between inner and outer Paris, traditionally divided by the lines of the old fortifications, has

122 become meaningless. The great housing estates and their huge, inhuman tower blocks have already crossed this one-time border and before long the peripheral arrondissements will be absorbed into the inner city suburbs. The core of the city is still holding out, but architectural chaos creeps closer day by day. At this rate, by the year 2000, our children will be left with nothing but a few pieces left over from a jig-saw puzzle, which will have no meaning, no reality for them because of the wanton destruction of a beautiful city patiently created by centuries of unremitting labour. And it has only taken twenty years to do all this irreparable damage!

Obviously the city had to be rebuilt after the Liberation, to try to ease the housing crisis and cope with the enormous growth in the volume of traffic. Some-

thing had to be done to ensure that this vast metropolis — 20 % of the population crammed into 2 % of the national territory — could function efficiently. What could be done in the face of the massive congestion caused by a prolonged period of centralization? The

The spacious open squares at the Défense, where the first of the great urbanisation schemes is nearing completion.

only answer was to build. So, since the beginning of the fifties, we have been building, anyhow, anywhere. The essential thing was to build, and build quickly, to provide people with homes and keep the traffic flowing. Never mind if the materials are not quite up to standard; everyone knows that the work is only guaranteed for ten years! Never mind the quality of the architecture — just put up as many blocks of flats and skyscrapers as you can and cover the lot with concrete! Who cares if the result is ugly and characterless? Never mind where you build either! Don't worry about the quality of life of the people who are going to live out there in the suburbs — we'll build them shops and schools and a metro station later. The only thing that matters is quantity.

Recently however, it must be admitted, a perceptible effort has been made to take aesthetic values into account, and the housing built in the last few years has shown a marked improvement on earlier development. But as long as the property boom goes on, and the constant demand for more and more houses, more and more roads keeps up the pressure for this savage expansion, the city will continue to build, build and then build! Even if it ruins Paris in the process.

Today even the inner areas of Paris are in danger. Concrete cubes are springing up all over the place. Belleville, Maine-Montparnasse, Italie are all inner suburbs which have already been "renovated". They may well be eliminating the last few really insalubrious spots in the city, but they are certainly destroying the warm neighbourhood faubourgs and creating ever more zones of isolated anonymity in the tortured capital. Here and there isolated projects have succeeded — brutally quickly — in destroying some of the few remaining treasures. The famous "hole" of the Halles has been left gaping at the feet of Saint-Eustache for far too long now. Baltard's arcades which once stood there, a fine testimony to the metal architecture of the Second Empire, are nothing but a nostalgic memory, and the only people to profit from this sacrilege are the businessmen

Beaugrenelle — one of the most recent of the vast commercial centres, on the left bank of the Seine in the 15^e arrondissement.

who have turned Zola's *Ventre de Paris* into yet another hypermarket.

What was once a lovely view along the Seine from Bercy to the Etoile, is now completely ruined. As we look downstream from the quays we see first of all great office blocks dwarfing the lovely 19th century tower of the gare de Lyon; then come the clumsy-looking administrative buildings of the city of Paris (a fine example the city fathers set!) and the impersonal bulk of the cité des Arts followed by the huge buildings of the new science faculty; and most of all, well before we reach the characterless luxury of the Champs-Elysées, there is the right-bank expressway, thanks to which the quays and river banks have all disappeared, and with them the starry-eyed lovers, the patient fishermen and the painters who used to frequent them. Small wonder that cars rush by here without slowing down; there is nothing of interest or beauty left to see. Still, I suppose we should count ourselves lucky that plans for a similar scheme along the left bank were shelved, together with an attempt to

123

The Défense in close-up... out ▶ beyond the Arc de Triomphe, this is where the eye comes to rest when we look up that long straight vista from the Louvre.

126 bring the motorways right into the heart of the city by means of a series of radial link-roads. Either of these plans would have totally destroyed the capital — we have only to look as far as Lyon for proof of that!

And what has happened to the Paris landscape amid all this? There is an aesthetic value in the design and lay-out of a town which is almost as important as that of the buildings themselves. The imaginative use of urban space, the planning of lovely vistas and of vantage points from which to view them, the relationship between the size of buildings and the distance they are apart — all this is what makes or marks a beautiful city. Paris has always been rich in all these ways, and one would have thought such riches were worth preserving. But the example of other capitals, Prague and Rome for instance, where the necessary highrise housing has been kept out of the city centre, has been ignored. In Munich and Vienna, historic sites have been protected, and the volume of traffic in the city centre has been kept down by the creation of large-scale pedestrian precincts. Paris has largely chosen to ignore this successful experiment too, and happily goes on destroying irreplaceable buildings and lovely views alike. What do we see as we look out over the Arc de Triomphe from the Louvre? The towers of the Défense! As we look up the esplanade towards the facade of the hôtel des Invalides, what do we see looming in the distance? The monstrous tour Montparnasse! And on the horizon, beyond the trees of Montsouris? Towers, more towers, towers everywhere! Even as we wander through the heart of some of the oldest parts of the city, we find the same thing — everywhere new blocks have crept in among the old, breaking the harmony and disfiguring everything to the point where the streets are becoming corridors for fastmoving traffic flowing between the barren walls of a dehumanized world. This sickness is already well advanced on the Champs-Elysées and it is gradually spreading to the broad avenues of Auteuil and Passy. On the *boulevards extérieurs* it has reached an almost terminal stage.

Will anyone ever be able to cure it?

Paris and its contrasts... futuristic tower-blocks and intriguing metal mobiles on the water-front of the Seine (Beaugrenelle).

3

living in Paris

*Outside a fashionable restaurant
in the faubourg Saint-Germain.*

a permanent world fair

F OLLOWING THE EXAMPLE of the other great capitals of the world, Paris since the reign of Napoleon III, has held a great number of international exhibitions: 1855, 1867, 1889, 1900, 1937... The list is long and not yet at an end for another world fair was planned for 1989 as part of the celebrations which will mark the bi-centenary of the French Revolution.

Each time, the State and the city of Paris have honoured the occasion by building a new monument, transforming an existing one or creating something of lasting value to the life of the city. Thus we owe the Tour Eiffel to the 1889 exhibition, the Grand Palais and the metro to that of 1900, and the Palais de Chaillot, which replaced the old Trocadero, to that of 1937. Other "wonders" were only erected as temporary displays, so they have long since disappeared from the scene together with most of the foreign exhibits which were often remarkably exotic or extravagant. Two of these are still with us: the Palais du Bardo, a replica of the Bey of Tunisia's residence, built for the 1867 exhibition and rebuilt stone by stone in the parc Montsouris; and the Chinese pavilion from the 1900 exhibition which under the name of La Pagode has become one of Paris's famous avant-garde cinemas.

But Paris herself, every single day of the year, is like a permanent world fair, with thousands and thousands of exhibits covering every inch of the city. Just imagine how long it would take to visit them all and look at everything there is to see! Many of the five million foreign tourists who visit Paris every year only

stay for two or three nights, just long enough for a coach tour of the sights and a sample of Paris night-life. Obviously, if you want to see the real Paris you will need to stay much longer — a week simply to realize how big the city is, a month to get to know her, and perhaps a whole life-time to reach the heart of this unique town which is like a universe in itself.

Once you have visited all the usual monuments: the Pompidou Centre (five million visitors a year), the Eiffel Tower and the Louvre (three million visitors each), Napoleon's tomb (one and a half million) and a few of the other museums and monuments included in all the organized tours of the capital, it is worth spending some time merely watching the people around you. Life in Paris goes on in so many different guises that it can

seem like a microcosm of the whole world. A very high proportion of the most important elements, the moving forces of French life, are located here in these 2,600 hectares which the playwright Giraudoux called "the most thought about, the most talked about, the most written about" in the world. I would only add "and the most lived in..."

The figures speak for themselves. Paris accounts for 11 % of France's trade, 33 % of her bookshops and cinemas, 15 % of her alcoholic consumption, 90 % of her jewellery business... Paris has never been a closed society, and she has always welcomed people of every colour and creed who come to savour her food and drink, to amuse themselves or to absorb her culture, to buy their clothes, to see her sights or simply to wander through her avenues and parks and just dream! For after all, Paris has something for everyone with her 1000 restaurants, 8000 cafés, 2500 auction sales every year at the hôtel Drouot, 331,000 little artisan workshops or studios, dozens of libraries and museums, her 80 theatres, 300 art galleries and 465 cinemas.

There is no need for great world fairs or international congresses, nor even for the thousand and one exhibitions and fairs of one sort or another which constantly fill the Palais des Expositions at the porte de Versailles, or the C.N.I.T.

Another study in contrasts... An elegant boutique in the faubourg Saint-Honoré.

pavilion at the Défense, to entertain the waves of visitors — tourists and workers, folk from the suburbs and the provinces, and the foreigners who all pour into the city every day. Each day, in fact, more than a million people travel in to work from the suburbs by car or bus, train or métro; and once they arrive in town there are more trains, cars and buses ready to ferry them around. If you think of these arrivals on a yearly basis you arrive at an astronomical figure. 22 million arrive by plane, 70 million take taxis, 312 million take buses or trains and more than a billion use the métro! These figures include the four million Frenchmen who visit their capital each year, and the five million foreigners who between them occupy the 140,000 hotel rooms in Paris — over half the number in the country.

For the tourists, every day is filled with coach trips and guided tours of some of the 333 monuments in the city. But the only real way to appreciate Paris is to discover it alone. Just dive into the hubbub of the crowded streets if you want to get to know the places we have visited on our journey round the city. As our inventory of its treasures has shown, they are very unevenly distributed among the twenty arrondissements. You will have noticed that the vast majority are inside the old fortified walls of the city, as the maps at the end of the book show. The way people live and the work they do can also differ from one district to another, for several of the trades or professions have shown a marked preference for one particular part of the city. Sometimes it may be a whole arrondissement, sometimes a single street, but a tradition has been created there, and lent the district a special colour. Often the pattern has been broken when there have been mass migrations of population which have changed the old order completely. In the old "villages" south of Paris for example, the traditional crafts have been swept away by large-scale property development. And elsewhere, particularly in and around the Champs Élysées, office blocks have gradually taken over the avenues and boulevards

One of the enormous department stores on the boulevard Haussmann.

the old traditional links between the trades and professions and the districts associated with them have survived. The 7ᵉ (boulevard Saint-Germain) is still the diplomatic quarter; the bankers are still mainly in the 9ᵉ (boulevard Haussmann); the newspaper offices in the Champs-Élysées and in the 9ᵉ; and the tailors' and dressmakers' workshops in the 2ᵉ and 3ᵉ (the Sentier district). Thus behind the boulevard Voltaire, in the Marais and the Sentier, at the Bac-Raspail crossroad, and at Richelieu-Drouot, we can find ourselves

plunged into a series of completely different and self-contained miniature worlds. For instance, we could "do" the rue du Faubourg-Saint-Antoine to find its cabinet-makers and carpenters, or the rue de Paradis looking for porcelain and cut-glass ware. The rue de Sèvres, rue de Passy and the rue du Faubourg-Saint-Honoré have their exclusive dress shops and the rue de Seine its art galleries. And so on...

We could again let tradition or fashion be our guide and consider how, from the 18th century onwards, one district after

129

another in turn became the fashionable and exclusive area of the moment, the one place where everyone who wanted to be *dans le vent* either lived or had to be seen out walking and meeting his friends. In their turn the Palais-Royal, the Champs-Élysées, the Chaussée-d'Antin, Montmartre, Montparnasse and Saint-Germain-des-Prés have all been given the coveted accolade of *le Tout Paris,* and their restaurants, cafés and theatres have been the fashionable rendez-vous of the smart set. In those days fashions and trends tended to last for several years at a time. It is all very different today when a particular restaurant, night-club or boutique becomes the four-star attraction of the moment. For at the end of each season — and a single season is the normal lifetime of a modern fashion — another star will rise in the firmament and in its turn disappear too. But naturally of course, the great business centres, theatres like the Opéra or the Comédie Française, and famous restaurants like the Tour d'Argent never lose their popularity however fashions in general may change.

In this busy crowded capital you can find everything you need, everywhere. And, just as the provinces are no longer a desert compared to Paris, so in the same way the peripheral *arrondissements* and out-of-the-way suburbs are

now almost as well equipped as the centre. Cinemas showing the latest films, drugstores, ready-to-wear shops and exotic restaurants are springing up all over the place. And oddly enough, at the end of this 20th century which has been so dedicated to modernization and progress, many of the little old-world 19th century restaurants in these suburbs which were once villages, have been rediscovered and are enjoying a great wave of popularity. Thus the whole city shares in this incessantly bubbling activity which is the hallmark of a great metropolis.

So let us join in the fun and take to the road! We shall not plan our route, but set off at random. The rules of the game are simple: take a road, any road (it should not be difficult for there are 5,300 of them), and see what you can find there in the way of shops, little squares and famous buildings. There is bound to be something of interest, and when you have exhausted your first choice, go on to the next one and so on... One other guideline: you will be able to take your bearings from any one of the 120 churches (most of them beautiful buildings); the 380 *colonnes Morris* (the pillars where lists of forthcoming attractions are advertised); the 340 kiosks (most of which sell newspapers, the odd one sells flowers); or the 137 fountains in the capital (an excellent

Paris has more than a thousand restaurants: some, like the Tour d'Argent (top left) and Maxim's (opposite page) are inordinately expensive...
Spilling out on to the pavements have been appearing, like this one near the Pompidou Centre.

pretext to have a rest, and if the water is not drinkable, there is always a café round the corner). So, make your own route, the city is at your disposal, you can do what you want to do, when and where and with whom you want to do it.

Is it time to eat? The choice is staggering, from the little restaurant with a *menu à prix fixe* to the gastronomic splendour of the Tour d'Argent. There is no need to feel limited to the *steak-frites;* you can eat anything you like, dishes from anywhere in the world: *sauerkraut, paëlla, bouillabaisse, chop suey,* or chicken Maryland. Whereas at mid-day the bistros are full of business men and women, all in a hurry to eat, at night under the soft candle-light the same bistros become the perfect setting for a romantic *dîner à deux.* In between times there are the *salons de thé* — if you want to dance you will have to go to the Coupole — and the café-bars — if you can put up with the canned music! Do you feel the urge to pray? There are temples, synagogues and a mosque. Or to visit a museum? There are museums for everything, from posters to impressionist art; from ceramics to sculpture; from hunting to aviation; from toys to precious jewels. Just name it, there is a museum which specializes in it! Inevitably, among so many collections some merit a special mention: for example, the Cernuschi museum of oriental treasures in the parc Monceau, the Guimet collection of Indian art, and the Balzac, Delacroix, Gustave Moreau and Victor Hugo museums which are housed in the artists' or writers' own homes. Then there is the Pompidou Centre, or the Carnavalet museum to brush up on your history of Paris, or the musée de l'Opéra if that appeals. And for light relief, we must not forget the musée Grévin with its amusing wax-works and its distorting mirrors which bring back all the fun of the old-time fairs.

We could make another whole, astonishing, inventory, but we must be content with just a short list: English bookshops, the bears at the zoo, the Indian shops, the wine shops, picture shops, joke shops, the dress-hire shops, where we can rent a dress suit and bow tie for gala occasions, the little donkeys in the Luxembourg gardens, the oriental pâtisseries, the judo and karate clubs, the bowling alleys, the skating rinks and the swimming pools... It would take a life-time to exhaust all the possibilities of this magical city. ∎

132   # *some other views*

WHEN YOU HAVE BEEN WALKING arm in arm with a woman you love, have you never wanted to pull away from her for a moment in order to see her better? A beautiful city must also be seen from a little way off, for it is from a distance and from different angles that we can best appreciate her face and the lines of her body.

We spoke earlier of the views from the surrounding hills as we came into Paris from the suburbs. But there is no need to go so far afield, and no need either to take an aeroplane and view her from above to be able to admire the extent and superb layout of this city. The *boulevard périphérique* is the perfect vantage point. These thirty-five kilometres form the outer boundary of Paris, beyond the *boulevards extérieurs.* Even if the gap is only a hundred metres or so in places, we are far enough away to see whole sectors of the city across the intervening space. So let us begin on the Ivry viaduct, looking down over the plain of the

13ᵉ arrondissement, a mosaic of buildings and railway lines stretching away to the Seine. Then, as we circle the *18ᵉ* between La Chapelle and Clichy, we get splendid views of the Sacré-Cœur. And as we follow the boulevard round, we can clearly see the different types of construction: brick from the thirties, dirty concrete from the fifties, nowadays modern steel and glass.

Inside the city there is no shortage of view points either. We can go up to Montmartre or to the Buttes-Chaumont, or better still to the top of one of the many tall buildings. As they are part of the very fabric of the city, we can look down and get a clear bird's eye view of everything below us. How much we shall see will depend on where and how high up we are. With a zoom lens, we could begin at the top of the tour Montparnasse or the Eiffel Tower and take in the whole city and even the hills beyond. From Notre-Dame or the Arc de Triomphe, we could shorten the range and focus on the pattern of the nearby streets and buildings. From the top of the Pompidou Centre we could almost touch the chimney-pots and TV aerials, for we should only just be clear of the surrounding houses. From almost any top floor flat in Paris, you can see that lovely tangle of rooftops and church spires, which must have looked so much more beautiful when there were no ugly modern buildings to spoil the view.

At the other extreme, if we go down instead of up — into the "basement" of the city — we shall get interesting glimpses of a quite different kind. Here is a whole series of fascinating underground worlds, whose existence we are hardly aware of at street level because their entrances are usually hidden by manhole covers or thick heavy gratings. A journey beneath the city takes us into another universe, even when we merely go as far down as the familiar escalators and tunnels of the metro. But when we are swallowed up in the vast echoing chambers of the R.E.R., we feel as though we are penetrating into some terrifying metal metropolis of the future. And if we go

down into the tunnels of the sewers of Paris, long underground rivers will take us into a fantastic world where we can quite easily believe in a dark lake beneath the Opera House complete with its phantom and its legends. Then, perhaps most macabre of all, we could visit the Catacombs, those ancient underground caverns — they were actually once quarries — which contain the remains of thousands of anonymous corpses whose skulls and bones line the galleries and leave an eerie and unforgettable impression on the visitor from the world above.

Let us work our way back to the surface now, to the fresh air again. The easiest way up is to take the escalator from one or other of the metro stations. In fact these moving stairways offer yet more vantage points and show us the city from other and often unusual angles. Just try the exits opposite the Arc de Triomphe, Saint-Germain-des-Prés or the Seine.

And talking of the Seine, can you imagine a great capital city without a river? With very rare exceptions the two go together, and Paris is the perfect example of this, for the life of the city is inextricably linked with that of her river. Born of the Seine, Paris lives with her parent river all along both sides of the thirteen kilometres they have in common. The river is very much in the heart of the city

A look at old-world Paris... Its old passageways...

A traditional artisan workshop.

— we have only to look at the number of bridges for proof of that. There are thirty-three of them in all, from the pont National in the east to the pont du Point-du-Jour in the west. The bridges themselves reflect the history of the city, from the 16th century Pont-Neuf to the most recent concrete viaducts. Each bridge has its own special characteristics: there is the beautiful classicism of the pont de la Concorde, the charming turn-of-the-century lamps on the pont Alexandre III, the poetic appeal of the pont Mirabeau, the popular zouave of the pont de l'Alma — Parisians check the level of the river by keeping an eye on him and once the water came right up to his chin!

Each one of these lovely bridges makes its contribution to the overall beauty of the city. As we stand on their parapets, we could never tire of the superb views they offer us. Views over the Ile Saint-Louis, which looks like a ship at anchor in its harbour, near enough for us to touch it almost; over the point of the Ile de la Cité when the setting sun colours the buildings on both banks so that even the skyscrapers lose something of their obtrusive ugliness; over the quays themselves and the water — in spite of the interminable streams of cars. Sadly, the river-buses no longer ply up and down the Seine, but at least the *bateaux-mouche* enable us to glide

along the river and see the facades of the great buildings. If we stroll along the banks we may still come across the odd *bouquiniste,* a few amateur painters and an old fisherman or two — and a few people just strolling along like ourselves. The riverside expressways have robbed us of many of the quiet backwaters we used to enjoy, but if we walk along the pavements raised above the quays we can still catch odd glimpses of the city between the trees. ■

133

a few special addresses

THE SHEER IMMENSITY OF PARIS can sometimes deter the tourist from wandering too far afield in case he gets lost in its labyrinthine tangle of little streets and its complicated transport network.

But despite the noise, the traffic and the crowds, there is a pattern in this apparent jumble of streets and buildings, and Paris today is no longer the maze it was in the Middle Ages. Many of its tortuous intersecting alleyways and narrow

Or this renovated, old-fashioned shop which seems to come straight out of grandma's day.

streets have disappeared, as one after another of the old parts of the city have been pulled down or restored, leaving the clear-cut lines of modern Paris plainly visible.

The secret places beloved of the real connoisseur, whether he be a native of the city or a discerning visitor, are now just a handful of special addresses in his notebook, addresses of places which the hordes of tourists who flock through the city have never even heard of. One may be the address of a particular bar, where an old pianist plays on until five o'clock in the morning; another that of a restaurant where you can eat an excellent *feiojada* for your Saturday lunch and listen to people playing and singing the samba all around you. Or yet again, you may have discovered a new *café-théâtre*, or a tiny shop where they sell remnants of silk at bargain prices. Every true lover of Paris has in his address book or in a secret corner of his mind his own private list of these special places to visit.

As we have covered most of the ground on our original voyage of discovery and visited most of the tourist "musts", why don't we have a look at some of them again, more closely this time to see if they have any secret corners that we have not discovered. There are unexpected treasures in many of the museums which we could quite easily miss. For instance, not everyone goes down to the basement of the Orangerie where Monet's great 'Nympheas' paintings fill the whole length of the walls, or visits the rear gallery of the Petit Palais to see the permanent collection of 19th century paintings, or lingers over the fascinating exhibition of model ships in the vast airy halls of the Musée de la Marine. Hundreds of such delightful discoveries await the inquiring visitor to Paris's many museums.

The Louvre, famous and much-visited as it is, offers extra bonuses to those who know how to look for them. Forget about the stars of the show, the Venus of Milo, the Victory of Samothrace and the Mona Lisa, that unrivalled superstar who, like all modern celebrities, now shelters behind a protective bullet-proof screen, and let the Louvre take you on a journey back to the dawn of civilization. Plunge down (literally, for they are on the lower floors) first into ancient Egypt and Mesopotamia, then travel up via the world of Greece and Rome, until you finally find yourself following the development of western art up to the time of Courbet and his contemporaries. You have passed through at least three layers of the history of man since you went two storeys down an hour or so ago — and all the time you could see through one or other of the windows the trees and flowering shrubs in the gardens outside and the waters of the Seine flowing calmly past only a few yards away.

Now go to some old parts of the city, where the narrow streets are like so many "real life" museums, and the past lives on to the present day. Passages and covered galleries run from street to street between the blocks of 19th century buildings, and names like passage des

Bizarre or unexpected sights too... like the elaborate tombstones in the Paris cemeteries. Here the inventor of the Pigeon lamp reposes in the cemetery of Montparnasse.

These walls encrusted with skulls and bones in the Catacombs.

Panoramas, galerie Vero-Dodat, passage Jouffroy, reveal charming old-fashioned shops and restaurants. The sculpted decoration of their upper storeys, the dilapidated windows and the general air of decrepitude behind the pillars of every doorway tend to make the passer-by think that he has stumbled accidentally into the set of some period French film. Sadly though, these calm oases are becoming fewer and fewer, and are all the more precious amid the ever-increasing noise and bustle of the modern world.

However, we can still find plenty of havens of peace and tranquillity out in the open under the Paris sky, and the Ile Saint-Louis, to which we have often referred, is one of them. We don't need the added attraction of Berthillon's famous sorbets and ice-creams to bring us here to stroll among its grand 17th century *hôtels particuliers* with their noble facades. It is hard to decide which is more pleasant — to wander round the island itself or look at it from the neighbouring quays. Although bridges link it to both banks of the Seine, this is

truly an island, remote from the pressures of mainstream Paris, going its own well-ordered way and clinging to a totally different lifestyle from that of the rest of Paris. There is another little "island" too, on the west of the city, the man-made allée des Cygnes, which also reminds us merely by its peaceful, tree-lined presence, of the simple pleasure of quiet walks in a green countryside.

On the slopes of Ménilmontant lies another vast green park twice as big as any of the Paris gardens. And although it enjoys splendid views over Paris, most people come simply to stroll among its shady trees and enjoy its deep silence, for the only sound here is the song of birds. This is the Père Lachaise cemetery. A cemetery, yes, but one where the sorrow of death is softened by the presence of nature. Many families have someone buried here and the cemetery is still in use, but sympathy with the bereaved is mingled with the thrill of meeting the ghosts this place enshrines. For Chopin is buried here, and his memorial stone is still covered every day with fresh flowers. Here too are Héloïse and Abélard, Molière, and Alfred de Musset too, who sleeps in the shade of the willow tree he asked for in his last poem. A favourite corner of Père Lachaise for the historically-minded Parisian is the *Mur des Fédérés,* part of the outer wall of the cemetery where a simple plaque remembers the 147 *communards* who were executed there in 1871 after vainly fighting their way across the graves. There are ordinary people here too, whose monuments or simple headstones with their tender, romantic inscriptions seem to endow the cemetery paths with a presence

which springs from the very earth. Here the noise of the great city seems a long way off, closing-time is forgotten until we are reminded of it by the *gardien's* bell — and we tell ourselves that next time we come we must remember to come in and leave again by the little door in the wall at the corner of the aptly named rue du Repos.

Green leaves, silence and water seem to be the essential properties of all these quiet oases, and it is once again these same ingredients which give our final walk along the canal Saint-Martin its charm. For this quiet waterway seems out of place in the concrete context of Paris. The sight of a canal right in the heart of the city is a timely reminder that Paris, built on the banks of a great river, is less than two hundred kilometres from the sea and is in fact a busy commercial port. The canal joins the Seine near Austerlitz, crosses the Arsenal basin, goes underground for about 200 metres beneath the place de la Bastille and the boulevards of the *11e arrondissement,* and resurfaces near République to link up finally with the docks on the canal de l'Ourq beyond the Villette basin. Along its tree-lined route, with its iron bridges, its locks and weather-beaten barges, it evokes the robust atmosphere of a pre-war French film along with the rural calm of a provincial waterway. What a miracle it is to find such an island of calm amid the warehouses and office blocks! And like the couples who come here to sit and watch the barges go by and the swing-bridges open and shut, we and the trees, the unhurried passers-by and the boatmen are all in a quiet world of our own. ∎

And just as unexpected, but on a gayer note, a barge on the Saint-Martin canal right in the middle of Paris.

Paris by night

NIGHT IS FALLING OVER PARIS... The last rays of the setting sun light up the huge glass dome of the Grand Palais, and twilight, which lingers so long in temperate climes, gently softens the outlines of the city. In half an hour — the statutory time lapse — the street lamps will be lit and motorists will switch on their lights; it is getting dark. But it is difficult to

realize it yet, for there is still so much light in the sky — the last tinges of sunset, the first stars and that permanent glow which comes from the city itself. In winter when night falls early, the homeward rush and all the traffic jams seem to eclipse the coming of the darkness. In summer though, night falls as late as ten o'clock when everyone is back at home and the streets are deserted.

The 14th July in the place de la ▶ Concorde when Paris is ablaze with floodlights and fireworks.

138 Whenever night falls it heralds the awakening of another world; another city rises out of the sleeping stones and the empty streets, another town with other people. Things that were so familiar in daylight take on a new aspect; even the motorists in their cars look more relaxed now they are out for pleasure instead of business, and all along the streets a strange complicity seems to spring up between all those who are not yet in bed.

Quite different from its daytime appearance, the city at night has just as many things for us to see and do, though these may vary as the night wears on.

21.00 hours: already much of the city is dead. In the shopping streets, the business quarters, the little squares which resounded with the lively hum of street markets earlier on — all is quiet now. The shops closed well before eight o'clock, leaving nothing but a dark, silent emptiness. In the residential districts, sleep is gradually taking over and before long the lights in bedroom windows will be going out one by one. Is this really the *Ville Lumière* we have heard so much about? The pale yellow circles of

light from the street-lamps do little to pierce the blanket of darkness that lies over the long deserted avenues. It is as if it were Sunday every night of the week with only a few delayed travellers hurrying home, or people walking their dogs round the blocks before bedtime. Apart from that — nothing! Blind windows look out over empty streets. Traffic lights perform their ritual dance of changing colours to car-less deserted thoroughfares. It is like some strange Venice in which the waters of the lagoon have been replaced by creeping darkness.

So much for quiet residential Paris! Elsewhere the city is very much alive, given over to the ephemeral pleasures which come to life at night. People are out for a night on the town! Restaurants, theatres and cinemas are the usual rendez-vous and their popularity follows the expected weekly pattern, working up to a climax of activity on Saturday night. It drops away to almost nothing from Sunday to Tuesday when everybody is recovering from the week-end, only to rise again as the cycle begins afresh. The eternal quality of Paris's night-life stems mainly from the passing traffic, the pale light from the street lamps, the flood-lit buildings and the glittering cascades of light from a thousand neon signs. Now is the time to look once more at those facades, those domes, the contours of those buildings we have seen by day, as they are picked out of the darkness by the magical beams of the floodlights. Old familiar landmarks are given a softer, slightly unreal appearance. Lights play on the fountains, ribbons of red and yellow lights wind up the Champs-Élysées, and the *bateaux-mouche* light up first one part of

the quays then another as they pass in the darkness. And finally there are the myriad little squares of light which turn every block of flats, every towering H.L.M. into a dazzling galaxy of chequerboard lights, hanging disembodied there under the stars.

Midnight. And night still looks like day. The people of Paris are out in the streets again, for the film has finished and most of the restaurants have served their last meals. How about one last drink before we go back home after a convivial evening spent with friends?

But the tourist coaches are still busy. After all the "culture" they have absorbed, these visitors are now in search of the lighter diet of "gay Paris" to round off their day. Still the same obligatory stops, the strings of enquiring tourists, the same stereo-typed reactions, but the cabarets and their plume-bedecked dancers now take the place of the museums and palaces they have visited during the day. Dinner at the Moulin Rouge or the Lido, a quick stop at the Folies-Bergère, then on to the Crazy Horse Saloon or the Nouvelle Ève — all included in the price of the excursion! And those places in Paris which lead a double life — the Champs-Élysées, the Grands Boulevards, Montmartre, Montparnasse — are as busy now as they were during the day. The cafés and restaurants here are still open, parking is impossible and the traffic is moving at a snail's pace.

02.00 Night is slowly catching up. Here and there places are beginning to close. Waiters are presenting the last bills, and starting to put the tables and chairs away. More and more lights are being switched off. The remainder of Paris prepares to sleep in the vast nocturnal graveyard. Up to now

Paris by night where the bright lights speak for themselves.
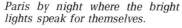

140 we have been able to enjoy a normal evening — dinner after a show, a visit to a night-club and one last drink. Now it is all over, even on the Champs-Élysées, in Montparnasse and Saint-Germain, even in the Forum des Halles.

03.00 Night has really taken over at last, the real night where only the most determined hard-liners are still out and about. There are still a few places where they can escape from the deathly quiet of the streets, a last few dingy bars where drinks and company can still be found.

In view of the savage reconstruction work being carried out on the face of Paris, this is probably a good time — in point of fact it is probably the only time — to walk along the streets and squares, through all those lovely nooks and crannies in the town, a town which at this time of night is yours alone. It is the man who walks by night who is the only real pedestrian in Paris. For him each stone becomes alive, each building reveals its true identity, each fellow-creature rediscovers his human warmth in this lunar landscape lit by the silent stars of a thousand street-lamps.

05.00 We cannot give up now — we must keep on to the end of this journey through the Paris night. We have walked for miles, dreamed of a thousand things, had a few drinks of course, and seen and heard everything — the transient friendship with a passing stranger, easy love, a few fights and those never-ending night-time conversations made up of exaggerated memories and dreams of unattainable Utopias. But isn't that what life is all about?

And at last we are almost at the end of our journey — and of the night! Only Montmartre and the Halles have not yet capitulated. It is there that we must go to see out the rest of the night, despite the sleazy bars and the ever-present ladies of ill-repute — but then, if they were not here, this would be as dead as the rest of Paris.

Night is fading and a new day is breaking. It is half-past five and the first metro of the day has just left. The first few early-morning workers are appearing, the first cars and lorries have started up, and the first pale gleam of day-light is beginning to creep through the thinning veil of darkness. It is time to have that bowl of onion soup in the Halles and indulge in the first cigarette and cup of coffee of the day.

And where better than from the Arc de Triomphe could we watch the rebirth of the city, the daily miracle which brings everything slowly back to life, the gradually lengthening perspectives of the Champs-Élysées at the end of which the solitary needle of an Egyptian obelisk slowly takes shape again before our eyes? ∎

Place Pigalle.
The towers of Notre-Dame de Paris at sunset.

The great Parisian tourist attractions

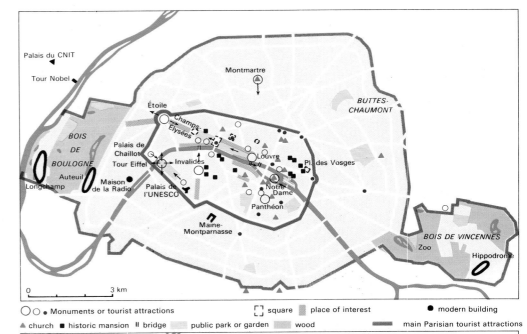

Palais du CNIT
Tour Nobel
Montmartre
BUTTES-CHAUMONT
Étoile
Champs-Élysées
BOIS DE BOULOGNE
Palais de Chaillot
Tour Eiffel
Invalides
Louvre
Pl. des Vosges
Auteuil
Longchamp
Maison de la Radio
Palais de l'UNESCO
Notre-Dame
Panthéon
Maine-Montparnasse
BOIS DE VINCENNES
Zoo
Hippodrome

0   3 km

○ ○ • Monuments or tourist attractions   ⊏⊐ square   █ place of interest   ● modern building
▲ church ■ historic mansion ‖ bridge   public park or garden   wood   main Parisian tourist attractions

Museums and art galleries

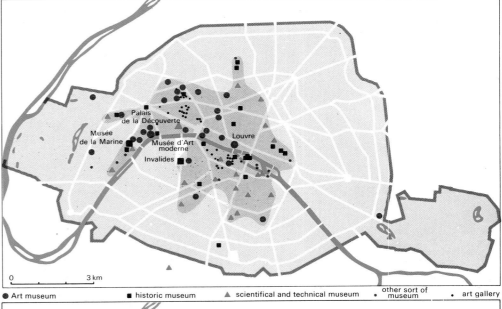

Palais de la Découverte
Musée de la Marine
Musée d'Art moderne
Louvre
Invalides

0   3 km

● Art museum   ■ historic museum   ▲ scientifical and technical museum   • other sort of museum   • art gallery

The shows

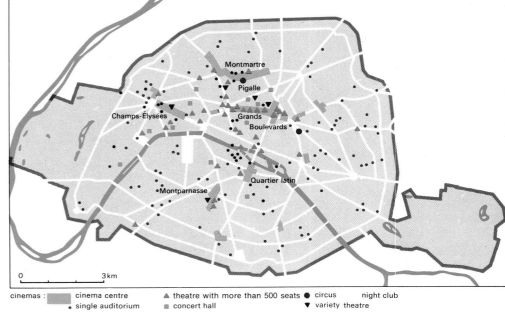

Montmartre
Pigalle
Champs-Élysées
Grands Boulevards
Quartier latin
Montparnasse

0   3km

cinemas :   cinema centre   ▲ theatre with more than 500 seats   ● circus   night club
• single auditorium   ■ concert hall   ▼ variety theatre

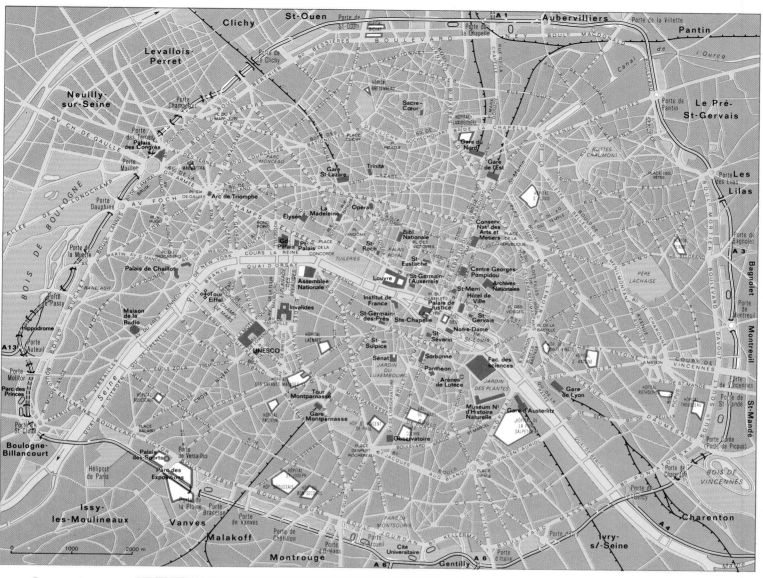

General map of Paris today

Extension of Paris from the XVIth century to the XIXth century

Legend:
- Philippe Auguste wall
- Charles the fifth wall
- fortfied wall
- Farmers General wall

1 - St-Martin-des-Champs
2 - St-Germain-des-Prés
3 - St-Victor
4 - Temple
5 - Louvre
6 - Monnaie
7 - Tuileries
8 - Palais-Royal
9 - Luxembourg
10 - Pont-Neuf
11 - Pont Notre-Dame
12 - Hôtel de Ville
13 - Place Dauphine
14 - Place des Vosges
15 - Palais de Justice
16 - Sorbonne
17 - Place des Victoires
18 - Place Vendôme
19 - Invalides
20 - Place de la Concorde
21 - Rue Royale
22 - Étoile
23 - St-Sulpice
24 - Panthéon
25 - Institut
26 - Notre-Dame
27 - Petit-Pont
28 - Pont-au-Change
29 - Pont-Marie
30 - Pont-au-Double
31 - Pont de la Tournelle
32 - Pont Royal
33 - Pont de la Concorde
34 - Pont des Arts
35 - Pont d'Iéna

Photographic credits

Pages 6 et 7, phot. : D. Barbier-Atlas Photo/Loucel-Fotogram. *Pages 8 et 9,* phot. : G. Champlong-Image Bank. *Pages 10 et 11,* phot. : L. Rousseau-Top/C. Rives-Cedri/L. Girard. *Pages 12 et 13,* phot. : F. Hidalgo-Top/A. Chambon-Vloo/O. Girard-Vandystadt. *Pages 14 et 15,* phot. : D. Barbier-Atlas Photo. *Pages 16 et 17,* phot. : R. Mazin-Top/J. Gabanou-Diaf. *Pages 18 et 19,* phot. : C. Sappa-Cedri/B. Hermann-Gamma/H. Gyssels-Diaf. *Pages 20 et 21,* phot. : R. Mazin-Top. *Pages 22 et 23,* phot. : L. Freed-Magnum/R. Mazin-Top/M. Folco-Gamma. *Pages 24 et 25,* phot. : R. Mazin-Top/E. Berne-Fotogram. *Pages 26 et 27,* phot. : S. Marmounier-Cedri. *Pages 28 et 29,* phot. : Rousseau-Top/ E. Erwitt-Magnum. *Pages 30 et 31,* phot. : B. Glinn-Magnum/C. Rives-Cedri. *Pages 32 et 33,* phot. : S. Marmounier-Cedri/ B. Hermann-Gamma. *Pages 34 et 35,* phot. : F. Mayer-Magnum. *Pages 36 et 37,* phot. : B. Hermann-Gamma/R. Mazin-Top/A. Edgeworth-Image Bank. *Pages 38 et 39,* phot. : R. Mazin-Top/J. Y. Ruszniewski-Vandystadt/Revault-Pix. *Pages 40 et 41,* phot. : E. Berne-Fotogram/G. Boutin-Pictor Int./J.-P. Tesson-Vloo/O. Garros-Fotogram. *Pages 42 et 43,* phot. : J. Pavloski-Rapho/D. Barbier-Atlas Photo. *Pages 44 et 45,* phot. : R. Mazin-Top/J.-M. Loubat-Vandystadt/J.-C. Pinheira-Top. *Pages 46 et 47,* phot. : J.-M. Loubat-Vandystadt. *Pages 48 et 49,* phot. : F. Bouillot-Marco Polo/R. Mazin-Top/L. Rousseau-Top. *Pages 50 et 51,* phot. : F. Bouillot-Marco-Polo. *Pages 52 et 53,* phot. : M. Riboud-Magnum/Loucel-Fotogram/J. Mounicq-Fotogram. *Pages 54 et 55,* phot. : L. Freed-Magnum/O. Garros-Fotogram. *Pages 56 et 57,* phot. : J.-P. Tesson-Vloo/X. Richer-Fotogram/L. Girard. *Pages 58 et 59,* phot. : Hermann-Gamma/Revault-Pix/F. Jalain-Top/Hermann-Gamma. *Pages 60 et 61,* phot. : J. Gaumy-Magnum/J.-C. Pinheira-Top. *Pages 62 et 63,* phot. : Revault-Pix/Hermann-Gamma/J.-C. Pinheira-Top. *Pages 64 et 65,* phot. : G. Boutin-Atlas-Photo. *Pages 66 et 67,* phot. : L. Rousseau-Top/L. Rousseau-Top/E. Berne-Fotogram. *Pages 68 et 69,* phot. : R. Mazin-Top. *Pages 70 et 71,* phot. : R. Mazin-Top/J.-Y. Ruszniewski-Vandystadt/R. Mazin-Top. *Pages 72 et 73,* phot. : R. Mazin-Top/D. Barbier-Atlas Photo. *Pages 74 et 75,* phot. : R. Mazin-Top. *Pages 76 et 77,* phot. : D. Stock-Magnum/J.-C. Pinheira-Top. *Pages 78 et 79,* phot. : R. Mazin-Top. *Pages 80 et 81,* phot. : B. Glinn-Magnum/L. Girard/J.-C. Pinheira-Top/G. Boutin-Pictor Int. *Pages 82 et 83,* phot. : C. Sappa-Cedri/R. Mazin-Top. *Pages 84 et 85,* phot. : L. Girard. *Pages 86 et 87,* phot. : J. Gabanou-Pictor Int./E. Lessing-Magnum. *Pages 88 et 89,* phot. : Lawson-Rapho/J. Wehrlin-Fotogram. *Pages 90 et 91,* phot. : B. Barbey-Magnum/Loucel-Fotogram/J. Ph. Charbonnier-Top. *Pages 92 et 93,* phot. : L. Rousseau-Top. *Pages 94 et 95,* phot. : Boeno-Pix/ R. Mazin-Top/Hermann-Gamma. *Pages 96 et 97,* phot. : F. Jalain-Top/L. Girard. *Pages 98 et 99,* phot. : J. Brinon-Gamma/F. Jalain-Top/J. Cochin-Vandystadt. *Pages 100 et 101,* phot. : J. Gabanou-Pictor Int./D. Burnett-Contact. *Pages 102 et 103,* phot. : G. Champlong-Image Bank. *Pages 104 et 105,* phot. P. Boulat-Cosmos/R. Mazin-Top/B. Glinn-Magnum/D. Czap-Top. *Pages 106 et 107,* phot. A. Froissardey-Atlas-Photo/R. Mazin-Top. *Pages 108 et 109,* phot. : G. Boutin-Explorer. *Pages 110 et 11,* phot. : R. Mazin-Top/Méry-Vloo/F. Bouillot-Marco Polo. *Pages 112 et 113,* phot. : L. Girard/L. Rousseau-Top. *Pages 114 et 115,* phot. : Chemin-Pitch/Larousse. *Pages 116 et 117,* phot. : Hermann-Gamma/F. Bouillot-Marco Polo. *Pages 118 et 119,* phot. : D. Burnett-Contact/J.-C. Meignan-Diaf/Larousse. *Pages 120 et 121,* phot. : Larousse/-J.-Y. Rusniewski-Vandystadt. *Pages 122 et 123,* phot. : P. Kérébel-Diaf/E. Berne-Fotogram. *Pages 124 et 125,* phot. : F. Hidalgo-Top. *Pages 126 et 127,* phot. : E. Berne-Fotogram/Hermann-Gamma. *Pages 128 et 129,* phot. : O. Garros-Fotogram/E. Berne-Fotogram. *Pages 130 et 131,* phot. : B. Glinn-Magnum/C. Sappa-Cedri/B. Barbey-Magnum. *Pages 132 et 133,* phot. : M. Cabaud-Fotogram/Hermann-Gamma/Hermann-Gamma. *Pages 134 et 135,* phot. : L. Freed-Magnum/J.-P. Bozellec-Vloo/F. Jalain-Top. *Pages 136 et 137,* phot. : D. Barbier-Atlas-Photo. *Pages 138 et 139,* phot. : E. Boubat-Top/I. Berry-Magnum/H. Chapman-Fotogram. *Pages 140 et 141,* phot. : F. Mayer-Magnum/R. Mazin-Top.

Maps number 1, 2, 3 and 5 are original maps devised by Roger Brunet.

IMPRIMERIE LAZARE-FERRY. — 75012 PARIS. — Dépôt légal juillet 1982. — N° de série Éditeur 12228. — 523102-C-Septembre-1984.
IMPRIMÉ EN FRANCE *(Printed in France).*